DEAR ENEMY

by

James Bacque
&
Richard Matthias Müller

DEAR ENEMY

A Fenn Publishing Book / April 2000

Copyright © 2000 by James Bacque & Richard M. Müller

Book Design: McGraphics Desktop Publishing Ltd.
Cover Design: Kathryn Del Borrello
Project Editor: Allison Reid
Publisher: C. Jordan Fenn

Publishing assisted with a grant from the
German Canadian Cultural Historical Foundation.

Fenn Publishing Company Ltd.
Bolton, Ontario, Canada

Distributed in Canada by H. B. Fenn and Company Ltd.
34 Nixon Road, Bolton, Ontario, Canada, L7E 1W2

The contents and subject matter contained herein are the written
expressions of the authors and do not reflect the opinions, or ideology
of the publisher, or publisher's representatives.

Canadian Cataloguing in Publication Data

Bacque, James 1929.
    Dear Enemy

ISBN 1-55168-146-X

1. World War, 1939–1945 – Prisoners and prisons.   2. Prisoners of
War – History – 20th Century.   3. World War, 1939-1945 – Atrocities.
I. Müller, Richard Matthias. II Title.

D805.A2B32 2000   940.5472   C00-930149-6

Printed and bound in Canada.

I think that all this striving after greatness and domination is idiotic, and I would like my country to take no part in it.

— A.J.P. Taylor

As far as I'm concerned, to be disputed is the only possible status for an author, even if the dispute is sometimes an annoyance.

— Heinrich Böll

Introduction

This book began in a prison camp. Richard Matthias Müller, a former Nazi, Wehrmacht soldier and member of the Hitler Youth, was put into an American prison camp at Remagen in the spring of 1945, where he almost died of starvation and exposure. In 1989, he read with great excitement about Remagen and other camps in a book, *Other Losses*,* that James Bacque had written. Richard was excited partly because the book revealed mass atrocities against prisoners, which he had suspected but never seen proven before, and because his later experience at the American camp Philip Morris in Normandy largely contradicted what he had suffered at Remagen.

They met through a friend at Bad Kreuznach in the summer of 1991. They played tennis, drank wine, walked, and talked on and on (in English) about the Second World War, the camps, the Cold War, Germany then and now, Canada, air raids, neo-Nazis, German guilt, the Holocaust, revisionism. Richard objected to some of Jim's prisoner death statistics and promised to send him a full critique of the book, which he later did. Thus their correspondence began, and flourished in discussions of the camps, of writing, and of German experience since 1945. Soon they realized that if they continued on this course,

---

* *Other Losses:* An Investigation into the Mass Deaths of German Prisoners at the hands of the French and Americans after World War II. Toronto: Stoddart, 1989: revised edition, Toronto: Little Brown, [Fenn] 1999. In Germany, the book appeared as *Der geplante Tod:* Deutsche Kriegsgefangene in amerikanischen und französischen Lagern 1945-1946. Berlin: Ullstein Verlag, 1989.

they would have a lot of letters that might interest others, because they were writing as friends, opening vast and *verboten* topics in a reasonable, generous way.

They kept on for four years. Richard came to Canada with Hilla, his wife, to visit Jim and his wife, Elisabeth, to play tennis, and to keep on talking – and writing. They agreed to keep their eyes on an eventual book. In 1995, Jim returned to Germany to promote his new book, *Crimes and Mercies* (*Verschwiegene Schuld*)*, and to do some final editing on his project with Richard at Richard's house near Monschau. Then came Daniel Goldhagen's book *Hitler's Willing Executioners*, and a couple of letters were added. The result is what you have in your hands.

Richard Matthias Müller, Aachen and Monschau, March 28, 1999,
James Bacque, Toronto and Penetanguishene, April 13, 1999.

A Note on the Text

The manuscript was written entirely in English, since Jim has primitive German, and Richard's English is expert. Jim and Richard co-operated on the editing, at Monschau and by e-mail. A few inadvertent slips have been tidied away, and some of the early correspondence about prisoner death statistics has been pruned because it was too technical. A few source notes have been added for the reader's convenience.

---

* *Crimes and Mercies:* The Fate of German Civilians under Allied Occupation 1944-1950, London and Toronto: Little Brown [Fenn] 1997. In German: *Verschwiegene Schuld:* Die Alliierte Besatzungspolitik in Deutschland nach 1945, Berlin: Ullstein Verlag 1995.

September 12, 1991

Dear Jim,

It has been some time since we met at Bad Kreuznach, when I promised to let you have a corrected version of my PoW report. However, I have not been lazy. Although I could not completely neglect my own book, *Normal-Null und die Zukunft der deutschen Vergangenheitsbewältigung* (Normality and the future of Germany's struggle with its past), the final draft of which is now more or less completed, I was so fascinated by *Other Losses* (*Der Geplante Tod*) that I spent many, many hours reading and rereading it and making notes, and this is the comment I'd like to offer to you.

Your argument, based on documents and reports, is — with a few exceptions irrelevant to the general results — faultless. I realize that you have been *forced* by the evidence to come to your conclusions regarding treatment and conditions in the American and French camps and the approximate number of dead in them.[1] As far as "treatment and conditions" are concerned, this seems to be acknowledged even by your detractors — who then go on trying to explain and justify them as unavoidable, if deplorable.

I was fascinated and at the same time slightly troubled by the recklessness with which you stake all on the Big Number. Was it necessary to tie the fate of your book explicitly to it? Supposing people do not believe your big numbers, or the book actually fails to pass the test of statisticians, wouldn't it be a pity to let the people responsible for the atrocities get off the hook so easily?

We inmates of Remagen did think that the way we were treated by the Americans was abominable. Only our belief that it couldn't possibly go on for long, certainly not after the May 8, 1945, made it at all bearable. And yet I, and others whom I talked to years afterwards, never consciously saw a prisoner dying or dead in Remagen. Just one I knew fell seriously ill, was taken to a hospital tent, and after release fell ill at home, dying six years later.

---

* SH-Verlag GmbH, Schernfeld, 1994.

1 There were two hundred American camps in Germany in the summer of 1945, with approximately ten cages in each camp. At peak, about 5.2 million prisoners were in captivity in American camps in northwest Europe. There were more than a million PoWs in Italy as well.

On the other hand, it is true that the bulldozing of sleeping prisoners that you mention as reported of Rheinberg also happened at Remagen. The absolutely reliable abbot of Siegburg, Johannes Heising, assured me of that recently. Interestingly, he had completely forgotten the event when he put his PoW-time report together, published in 1991. Only when a friend reminded him the other day did the thing come back to him in a flash.[2]

There is one more general point I would like to make. The overall tenor of the book is one of moral indignation at what some Americans and especially Eisenhower were capable of doing. That is in line with the attitude struck by the world of victors, victims, journalists, politicians, church ministers in the face of mass atrocities by others, at least since the crimes of Nazi Germany came to light.

Now, I'm very much in favour of truth being revealed — any truth — and I am regularly furious when an embarrassing piece of truth is being suppressed by interested parties and its potential revealers prevented from finding or telling it on the grounds that this would damage some good cause, profit "our" enemies, or obscure some much bigger evil. For the rest, however, and especially after the truth has been established, I am all for "understanding," for finding causes and extenuating circumstances, and all against hypermoral judgments by people without historical knowledge and imagination.

Everything Eisenhower did or allowed to happen I see in the context of an almost universal, if unacknowledged, desire for near-genocidal retaliation against Germany. When the Great Powers at

---

2 The incident is described in *Other Losses* (revised, ed. 1999) as follows: "The most poignant story about this comes from an ex-prisoner, Johannes Heising, formerly the abbott of a monastery on the Rhine. In the 1990s he published a book about his experiences in the US camp at Remagen. After the book was published, Heising was talking with another former Remagen prisoner, Franz-Josef Plemper, who reminded him of something Heising had not described in the book: one night, the Americans had bulldozed living men under the earth in their foxholes. Plemper described the scene to him: "One night in April 1945, I was startled out of my stupor in the rain and the mud by piercing screams and loud groans. I jumped up and saw in the distance (about 30-50 meters) the searchlight of a bulldozer. Then I saw this bulldozer moving forward through the crowd of prisoners who lay there. In the front it had a blade making a pathway. How many of the prisoners were buried alive in their earthholes I do not know. It was no longer possible to ascertain. I heard clearly cries of "You murderer.""

the Yalta Conference in February 1945 made a show of declaring that they would not "destroy the German people," they revealed what had been on their minds. Eisenhower was obviously one of many, secretly determined not to be swayed by weak-minded humanitarians from doing what they considered was historically necessary in the face of German incorrigibility. And, of course, he was about the only one still in a position to do it.

One last point: your psychological argument against the punitive treatment of German prisoners — namely, that revenge can never lead to improvement in the guilty — is sound enough. But if you base it on the assumption that the majority of the German soldiers in the American camps did in fact feel guilty — individually, or at least collectively — I think you're fantasizing.

R.

October 2, 1991

Dear Richard,

You say that my argument is faultless, that I was driven to conclude what I did. And then you say I was reckless in stating the Big Number. You can't have it both ways — which is it?

As for your point about moral indignation: I doubt that anyone who felt the impetus to do such work as mine, which had to have its foundations in the belief that Canada and the U.S., France, and Great Britain fought the war for certain ideals of liberty, decency, and justice could have gone on with the research and writing without feeling indignant. In fact, I have heard from many Germans that the book is remarkably calm. You must remember the sense of betrayal I felt as I saw all the ideals for which I believed my father, my sister, and my two brothers and many relatives and friends fought the war cast into shame and degradation. As for understanding, I leave that to later work. What was necessary in this work was to establish the truth. Several Americans have confessed their sins to me, on condition that I not reveal their names. Several have confessed and subsequently recanted when faced with a TV camera or tape recorder.[3] One German, Hans Goertz, had to be pushed hard into

---

3 One American, former private Daniel McConnell, brought a claim against the Department of Veterans Affairs for "post-traumatic stress disorder"

telling what he had concealed for forty-five years. And finally, because most of these people hid what they were doing, they also hid why they were doing it. So most of the work to be done there is speculation, unless further research uncovers some proof of motivation.

As for your defence of Eisenhower and his murderous policies (the atmosphere of the times), I completely disagree. One of the most violently terrible things about the Nazi murder of civilians — Polish, Jewish, Catholic, Gypsy, etc. — is that the victims were innocent. It matters not at all that some Germans hated them. It matters enormously that they were innocent, and were never tried, never even accused of any wrong except the "wrong" of being who they were. To stay within our best traditions — "innocent till proven guilty" — the Allies should have tried everyone. Given that this was impossible, they could have sorted out only the Nazis and imprisoned them. But we didn't even do that. We helped Nazis who were useful to us; we imprisoned people who plainly could not have been guilty: children, pregnant women, and so on. In other words, I think we must find Eisenhower guilty, and your point of "the atmosphere of the times" should apply only to the sentence that we should retroactively pass on him.

You also say in your letter that I fantasize about the attitudes and thoughts of the German prisoners, but without showing that I am wrong. Several Germans have in fact told me that this passage about German feelings of guilt being quashed by the treatment the Allies meted out to them was quite accurate.

I think that the phenomenon you are going through, denying that you consciously saw atrocities in the camp, is what I have already encountered in others. It is hard to believe in the worst actions of mankind, even when one has experienced them. My friend Wolf von Richthofen could not believe for forty years that the Americans intended to do harm to the prisoners. Heising could not remember seeing the bulldozer. This is why euphemism works, and is one step towards atrocity.

J.

suffered when he was ordered to take over a "hospital" at Heilbronn in 1945. The hospital was only a dying ground, McConnell says: he had no medical training, and he was forced to supervise mass burials of prisoners who had died under his control. He had been given no food or medical supplies to help them. McConnell was awarded a 100 per cent disability pension in May 1998.

January 18, 1992

Dear Jim,

You say that several Germans agreed with your interpretation of the feelings and attitudes of the German soldiers after 1945. That may well be so, and of course it is always up to you to decide whose judgment and recollections you trust more. But I for one simply don't believe that any but a small minority of German prisoners had any feelings of guilt in those days, national or otherwise. They were crestfallen, weary, they had lost, all their sacrifices had been in vain, and now the Americans instead of feeling any compassion with a defeated enemy could think of nothing but to drive that lesson home (*vae victis* — woe to the vanquished). It took ten or more years before a sizable number of Germans (including me) accepted any responsibility, let alone guilt with respect to "Nazi camps." The idea that the U.S. Army — not by way of vengeful individuals but as a policy — was out to punish them for misdeeds, even destroy them physically, was, I think, so far from their minds that they began to think up all kinds of excuses for the Americans, which you have such a hard time in believing.

In fact, for most prisoners who survived and were not handed over to the French, the memory of the starvation camps faded pretty quickly. The experience was overlaid and mellowed by the comparatively good times most of them had in the labour camps afterwards and by the disastrous situation they were released into in the Germany of 1946-47. In the end there were few hard feelings against the Americans left — after CARE parcels and the Marshall Plan and what the Russians did. Anti-Americanism was an early gut reaction to the failure of the Americans to live up to German fantasies about the Liberators (an anti-Americanism revived by a later generation in the face of the Vietnam War).

R.

January 31, 1992

Dear Richard,

I am astounded by your remarks about prisoners' experience being "mellowed" by slave labour. This does not accord with the many letters I have had from prisoners who were in those slave camps, which they uniformly detested and left immediately when freed. As far as I could tell, they hated the slave and the open-field camps and did not find that slavery mitigated the death camps.

As for the harsh conditions in Germany in 1946-50, these were caused more by the Allied policies than by the war itself. That the cruel Morgenthau Plan was implemented has been confirmed most recently and authoritatively by Ambassador Paul Nitze in his memoirs, just published. (He was a senior American official in Germany at the time.) It has also been confirmed by Morgenthau himself in an article that he wrote in 1946.[4] That the Plan was implemented shows that it was necessary — i.e., that Germany had enough strength and productive capacity in May 1945 to frighten the Allies and to get herself out of economic difficulties much sooner than the Allies wanted.

Probably there would have been no need for the Marshall Plan in Germany had it not been for the Morgenthau Plan.

Well, Richard, I am beginning to think that what actually happens in life is that people who wish to rule others try to impose a certain view of the world on everyone else. It doesn't matter what the view is, as long as it is wrong. Or at least not necessary. That is the essential. The view must be more or less insane, in the sense that it does not accord with fundamental laws of human and environmental life — i.e., love of family, the need to eat, to think, to create, to find out things, to preserve one's life, to have fun, and so on. Because they are primarily interested in power, they must use force to rule, since people do not need to be forced to obey what I am calling the fundamental or normal bent of life. Therefore, whatever they use power in the name of must not be normal or natural, otherwise they could not convince the ruled that there was any need for rule. You

---

4   Henry Morgenthau Jr., in the *New York Post*, November 24, 1947. With thanks to Professor Ralph Raico, State University of New York at Buffalo. The "Morgenthau Plan" called for the partition and de-industrialisation of postwar Germany.

don't have to order people to get married, have children, and love them. Evelyn Waugh wrote, "Politicians are not people who seek power in order to implement policies they think necessary. They are people who seek policies in order to attain power."[5]

Just think of communism, Hitler and Marx, the medieval Church, for examples. The Aztecs founded their society on the belief that the earth was held up by four pillars, and the gods had to drink human blood once in a while or the pillars would fall down. They conquered lots of people and went on like that for hundreds of years. They only gave way to superior (Spanish) violence, not to truth.

Anyway, it is precisely because the view is wrong that it must be enforced. So the powerful fear artists because they are hard to fool and love freedom. Imagine the comical oddity of the pope telling Galileo to obey the diktat about the sun going round the earth. What passes for virtue or virtues is simply someone with enough guts to speak the truth about common sense in the face of oppression. Gorbachev, for example, although he did not go far enough. The views of Jesus and Socrates are fundamentally just common sense. That is why they have lasted despite oppression. No one has ever imposed them by force or will because there is no need to force a man to drink who is already drinking. When the maniac tyrants in the Church wanted to crush opposition and rule by will and terror, they had to depart from Christ to invent new theologies and systems of belief-obedience. So in the name of Christ, the Church abandoned Christ and ceased to be Christian, as you see today.

J.

February 13, 1992

Dear Jim,

The differences between my views on labour-camp times from those of others you have met may have something to do with the fact that I refer exclusively to the "cigarette" camps (Old Gold, Philip Morris, etc.)[6] on French soil after the war, especially around Le Havre, for

5 *The Diaries of Evelyn Waugh*, ed. Michael Davies, Penguin, p. 783.
6 "cigarette camps": American GI camps in France, of different sizes, which were given the names of well-known cigarette brands. German soldiers were attached to them, during the war as working PoWs, in accordance with the

which I am pretty informed, not only from my own experience but because six years ago I made an attempt at collecting evidence on them. I was not suggesting that anybody preferred life in them to being sent home. But apart from the fact that the camps' mere existence was against international law, nobody could have found fault with the treatment of prisoners in them.

Interesting that you mention Galileo. The case is not at all "dated" or comical. The pope was an enlightened man, a great sponsor of the sciences and even of Galileo. What he asked of him was that he should keep the thing where he thought it belonged: in academe, and not upset the public's beneficial trust in the authority of the Bible, on which so much depended. Would you have thought that I would come across the same thing in the German *Historikerstreit* (quarrel of historians) that took place in the middle of the '80s. Ernst Nolte and three other historians independently decided that nearly forty years after the Second World War it was about time to leave the ruts of post-war thinking about Hitler, the war, and Auschwitz and take a fresh, unhampered look at the facts. Especially Nolte made a name for himself inside and outside Germany by stoutly and expertly maintaining that there was no hope of understanding Hitler and Nazism without taking communism as "elder brother" and model into account. Hitler, he undertook to prove, was not only impressed by the way revolutionary Russia dealt with opposing forces but actually decided to copy communism in that respect. Nolte ventured the hypothesis that save for the Bolshevik antecedents, Auschwitz would not have been in the cards. When the more general German public was informed of this in an article in the *Frankfurter Allgemeine Zeitung (FAZ)*, the philosopher Jürgen Habermas rang the alarm bell. Nolte and others of his ilk, he felt, ought to be stopped in their tracks before greater damage was done.[7]

I was far from convinced that Nolte was right, but I acknowledged his credentials as a historian and welcomed unprejudiced, original thinking in Germany, after Hitler had suppressed it so effectively.

Hague Convention, and up to two years after the war illegally, as unpaid slave labourers. They were kept in separate, guarded barbed-wire cages in the neighbourhood of their workplaces.

7 "Vergangenheit, die nicht vergehen will". (The past that won't pass). *Frankfurter Allgemeine Zeitung,* June 6, 1986.

I won't be going into the intricacies of the fight that ensued, which was anything but a mere quarrel among historians. What struck me then was how political and moral thinking about the recent past seemed to have taken on the form of an infallible church and its doctrines. As in the case of Pope Urban VIII, the main concern of the philosopher Habermas and the other leading "priests" of principled German thinking wasn't truth but that nobody, not even historians, should upset the established politico-moral applecart.

R.

February 25, 1992

Dear Richard,

I agree with you about the cigarette camps. Your account of them agrees with other accounts I have received. However, the camp at Cherbourg, for one, appears to have had two sections, one smaller one, which was okay, and a bigger one, which was horrible. The smaller one was okay because the PoWs there were used for labour unloading ships.

I have had long and bitter experience with TV journalists on this prisoner subject, in France, the U.K., Canada, Germany, and the U.S.A. These journalists have been mainly superficial and silly, and several of them have told outright lies about me and my work. When the first edition of Other Losses *was published, my editor and I were interviewed for a Toronto TV program. One TV journalist turned the interview into a hostile attack on me, and when my editor protested, another journalist on the film team told him/her, "You have to forgive Andrew; remember, he's Jewish," as if this gave him the right to insult and defame me. But if Andrew were really interested in protecting Jews against supposed neo-Nazis, which was the apparent reason for the remark, then he should welcome my work, because it demands that we in the West protect those who are minorities in our hands. But one has to conclude that Andrew was really only interested in revenge. Jews in Canada are already safeguarded by the friendship and trust of their fellow citizens, a fact that is publicly demonstrated in the extraordinary legal protection of Jewish history in our laws.*

In general, the TV guys, having done a few hours of research, and having done their best to discredit Germans, then abandon all interest in the subject. It doesn't matter to them that new information comes along. They don't cover it. Why? Because they don't care. Their attention has run out; they move on to something else. They almost never revisit a story to correct an error. They have no notion of correcting, so they have no notion what is correct. Truth is often regarded as an annoyance that gets in the way of what they want to do.

As for Galileo: you have much more belief in the need for authority than I do. We are certainly from different shores of the ocean. I do not see that the people needed to pay such a price in treasure, allegiance, or faith, to the pope or the Church in those days, or now. Perhaps your attitude depends on a strong belief that authority produces order, which I don't believe. I think that order is produced by a desire for order, which springs from a sense of its value and of its limits. Think of the disorder in science caused by the pope's suppressing Galileo. Think of the disorder consequent on the extreme order of Napoleon and Hitler.

J.

May 31, 1992

Dear Richard,

I have just returned from a month in Moscow. The Soviet archives, hidden for forty years, have revealed their treasures. It is amazing and wonderful that my book is fully corroborated by these sources. Now I wonder what tricks the Americans and Germans and French will get up to, trying to undo this new proof.[8]

I enclose a Note on the archival sources.* I know you will exult with me over the spectacular Russian evidence.

My observation about the Germans today is that their moral sense is not clear and natural because they do so little to defend themselves against lies told about them, or to accuse others of the atrocities that "The Other" committed against them. I find this abnormal, and I believe it augurs

---

* See *Crimes And Mercies.*

8 In the seven years since this was written, not one scholar in Germany, France, England, the U.S.A. or Canada has used or written about the immense collection of documents in the Soviet archives that prove the atrocity in the American and French camps. A professor in Austria has noticed them, only to attempt to discredit them.

poorly for the future of Germans precisely because it is not normal. It sort of goes beyond even Christianity, into dizzy realms of unreality. When I say Christianity, I mean most precisely the injunction that you should treat your neighbour as yourself, and love others as you love yourself. Anyway, what do you think?

J.

July 10, 1992

Dear Jim,

Well, the Russians! If one lives long enough, one will see wonders. What are you going to do with those interesting notes on archival sources? And with "German postwar surveys of the missing"?[9]

I find it difficult to talk to you about the Germans today, of whom I am one, although it's a subject I quite fancy but prefer to write books about. Only a book gives me half a chance of impressing someone who has deviating views, and so many, alas, hold views deviating from mine. It's a pity your German will hardly allow you to read what I wrote. It would tell you a lot about me and the Germans. But even my wife complains that it's too difficult to read. The pivotal term in it is in fact *moral normality*. But of course after something in the life of a person or a nation has gone thoroughly wrong, there is no simple and easy course to normality, as you and others seem to assume. It's a cliff-hanging business whichever way you look at it.

You should not equate your position regarding the truth about Allied behaviour toward German PoWs with a German holding the same position. Among the victors, yours is a morally rare position to take, while all too normal on the side of the defeated. But morals aside, the world is simply not prepared to credit a truth of this kind coming from Germans. It would have no positive effect but would add to the universal loathing of them, fired just now by their having regained something of their old dominance in the affairs of Europe. Nobody thinks that these unjustly lucky bastards have any need to

---

9 These were surveys conducted by the Adenauer government to determine how many German prisoners of war were still missing from home in 1949-1954.

settle old accounts or "defend" themselves, even if there should be some truth in what they say. And after all, apart from going to court, defending oneself, especially against lies, is never an enviable proposition. Even those bystanders with no particular axe to grind will think it rather a bore. America-bashing may gratify most people around the world, but certainly not with Germany in the lead. German-bashing will take precedence over American-bashing anytime.

And then, there are (aren't there?) enough nations around as it is, pestering the world with their particular views of events and the wrongs they suffered at the hands of somebody or other and crying for redress. The abnormality of the Germans in abstaining from this should rather come as a relief. I tend to discourage such abstention only with much caution.

Motives are, of course, mixed. There is morality, there is cowardice, there is apathy, there is the perversity of yourself falling for slogans you have bandied about a little too long. But couldn't there also be some unusual national wisdom acquired the hard way over the past fifty years?

R.

August 25, 1992

Dear Richard,

"Well the Russians," you exclaim. Well, indeed. The archival notes will appear in Crimes and Mercies.

I am glad that you do trouble to talk to me about Germany today. You think, talk, and write clearly. Couldn't you write a book on the Germans today for English readers? Or adapt your existing one? So much ignorance still exists, even hatred and dislike. Perhaps we could collaborate in a series of letter-like exchanges. I could tell you and the Germans the agony you have put us through and our pain at discovering how much of what went wrong (1914 to 1945 plus) was our fault too, and how it is damaging us to this moment. By "us" I mean of course Britain, France, Canada, and the U.S. I'm sure there is a need to explain us to you.

As for your moral normality, I wonder what you mean. Do you mean what is actually practiced (see Tolstoy, The Law of Love and the Rule of Violence*)? Or do you mean the general belief in morality, not always* *practiced, but usually approved, which could be summed up roughly as "Love your neighbour as yourself," plus "Do as you would be done by," plus "The greatest rules are, love God and love your fellow person"?*

I do not think that it will be easy for Germans to return to normal. All I say for the moment is, They are not normal. (Yourself excepted, of course.) That was for me a staggering discovery. That nearly the whole of a people has been so damaged that it will not defend itself, or see the truth or admit the truth, from guilt, is extraordinary. I do not know the way out, except the prescriptive Love.

But love must begin at home in the self with a natural desire to do well by oneself. The only way out of the trap that you Germans are in, that I can imagine, is to admit that your guilt includes ours. That is, if you like, a form of love. You will treat us as we treat you (guilty). Not in revenge of course, but in the simplest justice, which you could call the retribution of love. If the great teachers would have us give food to others for the same reason that we give it to ourselves, the exact parallel is that if you in guilt admit your faults and make atonement from concern for others, and if you do this because it is best for you to do it, you have a duty in concern for us to show us where we went wrong and to show us that the road to atonement that you followed was not the wrong one, and therefore we should follow it too. Not the only food for people goes in the belly.

And you can see, looking at the state of the West today, the incredible hypocrisy that is widespread, and the cruelties toward blacks, women, and native Indians in the U.S.A., Canada, and elsewhere, that there is need for soul food too.

We cannot avoid these faults and sins until we recognize them. And one way to do that would be to admit what we have done, and undo it. Which means Germany, among others. You may think, What does that matter now? Nineteen forty-five was so long ago. But it does matter: our terrifying militarism is based on a sense of moral superiority mainly because of our great victory over the Devil Hitler. Until recently, people in the U.S.A. smashed Japanese cars on the street or picketed German buildings, saying, "Who won the war, anyway?"

The Americans went to war in Vietnam partly so there would not be "another Munich." And Saddam Hussein was repeatedly called "another Hitler." The victorious generals were feted with tickertape on Wall Street in 1991 just as the Second World War generals were in 1945. Militarism is a great fact of life today and has been for centuries in all the countries that condemn Germany for its militarism.

Now that Germany is effectively demilitarized, you can say without hypocrisy how you have suffered from it both via your own stupid leaders and via ours. And if we can expose and get rid of the militaristic myths of the West, we can expose some of the other hypocrisies better, and deal with them.

Earlier in this century, the British, French, and Americans condemned militarism from atop the highest pile of plunder the world has ever known. Not all the plunder has been restored, not all the Western peacemaking has convinced Arabs, Russians, Chinese, Vietnamese, or many other people that we really mean it (in fact, I think we do). By really mean it, I mean we are willing to give up something precious to us in return for peace among others. That we have done before, and can do again. It is the part of the civilizing genius of the West, but how dimly it flickers most of the time. That the UN is one of the greatest achievements of that genius is a sufficient comment on its success to date.

It is fascinating to me to see how a whole people (German) has changed under pressure. We in Canada have not undergone such pressure. You personally have changed, as you have told me, and so have I. But your personal change was both personally-morally willed and forced by your political and economic circumstances, created by the war, whereas mine arose from art (when I went to France to write a book and found by chance the first evidence of the Allied atrocities).

Another subject that interests me is collectivization. We condemn it in Russia and in Hitler's Germany, but we ourselves were ferociously collectivized during the war, to the extent that we condemned the whole of the German people as guilty in 1945, and saw the whole of our own side as collectively victorious-superior-righteous. Yeah, righteous. And we still are. There were no Allied death camps, the historians try to say to this day, not because they have the proof but precisely because they have no proof for their case at all.

They say my evidence on deaths is all wrong, but they do not advance any evidence how many prisoners did die. Isn't that extraordinary? They cannot say how many did die, yet they know that such and such a number did not die. How could professional historians get into such an absurd position unless they were working from an a priori position, i.e., our moral superiority, which admits of no possibility of our committing atrocities. And of course, from the hills of Scotland, the farms of Ireland, the forests of Tasmania and Newfoundland, the hills of Quebec, the valleys of eastern America, the plains of the American West, and the veldt of South Africa come the screams and the gunshots, and the hoofbeats,

*and then the silence, the long silence that shows there is no evidence. It
has all been buried.*

*Or at least no evidence until, a decent interval having passed, it is
carefully disinterred and the poor victims, martyrs even, are admired for
their courage in how they opposed us. Just as long as no one alive in the
West, no mortal family, is accused of a crime, or tried for it, or deprived
of anything gained through it. No, no, we cannot have justice in this life,
but only when the page is turned.*

*So the "historians" say, "No, there was no such camp as you were in,
Richard, no such deaths as those around you, because there could not
have been." They have half convinced you, and they almost fooled Heising.*

J.

September 29, 1992

Dear Jim,

You vent the fascinating idea of us two collaborating in a series of
letter-like exchanges about Germany and the Western world, guilt,
love, and so on. Well, you would find me ready, if you were to see to
the technical side of it. Something like this was done in a weekly
feature in *Die Zeit* magazine pre-1989 between a West German and a
GDR writer, the former mainly critical of the Federal Republic, the
latter critical of the Honnecker state she was later forced to leave.

"Moral normality." The actual term in my book is "*Normal-Null,*"
which is the German expression for "mean sea level" (MSL), applied to moral judgment. As the fixing of an MSL is the precondi-
tion for making meaningful statements about the height of moun-
tains, I point out that moral judgments, too, require the fixing of a
scale, i.e., a point "0" from which upward or downward you measure
when pronouncing something morally unacceptable or good or great.
And this is not so much a requirement as an (often unacknowledged) fact of life. Every time you judge human behaviour morally,
you implicitly refer to some baseline. What is usually lacking is an
awareness of this and consistency in its application. I maintain that
societies, big or small, at any given time settle roughly for a common
baseline, again often without being aware of this and often splitting
it systematically according to whether it is applied to judgments

about themselves or about others. This is well known by the name *double standards.*

There is also at times a tendency for the real baseline to be obscured by the impact of moral ideals, as taught by visionaries, founders of religions, preached about in churches, schools, and ceremonial assemblies. People may be fooled into believing that these highly commendable ideals have replaced the more humble requirements of common decency. But as most human behaviour will still fall short of that exalted new zero line, the consequence is that most human behaviour then has to be called bad, and praise is out: one doesn't praise people for fulfilling mere obligations. This Manichean system may of course reflect reality in some rare individuals or select groups by whom moral excellence is nothing but duty, any falling-off from which constitutes guilt to be admitted publicly. But for most individuals and societies such a stance is nothing but delusion, confusion, or hypocrisy.

Run-of-the-mill morality centres on what people that "you and I" consider on a par with us do or don't do as a matter of course (and allow others to demand of them as a matter of course). What goes beyond will deserve praise, and only what is subnormal will constitute guilt to be censured by others. For in normal life, Normal-Null is not merely a theoretical line like MSL or zero temperature, it is also of a certain thickness, constituting something of a behavioural zone. Real saints of one kind or another, who acknowledge only Good or Bad with no grades and shades in between *when judging themselves* still do well — on moral and pedagogical grounds — to revert to the conventional baseline when judging *others.* They will promote higher morals by praising and rewarding the exceptional rather than by damning the average.

So much for a rough outline of my concept.

With regard to Germany, my contention is that the German government and a sizable number of other Germans — or if you like, "the" Germans "collectively" — behaved abysmally below normal between 1933 and 1945 — and that by any standard, including that of the Germans themselves. If the people are viewed individually, however, the overwhelming majority behaved even then within the band of normality, i.e., meriting neither praise nor reproach. It is only the enormity of the atrocities under Hitler that seems to make it impossible for the victims and the world to admit this. Even the biological disappearance of the Germans who lived in the time of Hitler and might share his guilt does little to stop the accusations levelled at present Germany. So much blood and suffering unreasonably goes on crying for an adequate number of perpetrators: to be despised and punished, or at the least admonished.

That touches on the topic of collectivism you deal with in your letter. This moral censure (or praise) of collectives I view as something irrational, inherited from the early days of our species, something still going strong, though discredited intellectually and morally: a fact of life to be reckoned with, but not to be upmarketed to a rational or moral or metaphysical status. When in late 1945 a GI in camp Philip Morris showed us the horror pictures of the German concentration camps in *Life* magazine and said, "We Americans have our tough guys too, but we never did anything like that," I said, "Neither did we," referring to the individuals he was addressing and (hopefully) most of the German people.

My second contention and subject proper of my book is that after 1945 to the present day, German governments, including the bulk of their respective political oppositions and all the decisive public forces in this country, especially the media, plus the German people voting for the said parties and electing these governments (or at least suffering them), provided a spectacle of admission of guilt and expiation that although falling short of what one may dream of, went definitely above and beyond anything the world has seen of nations guilty of awful crimes.

History shows that not-seeing, not-confessing, and not-expiating your guilt is normal in the guilty. Normal behaviour of such nations and groups is concealing, denial, making counteraccusations.

On the other hand, of course, the normality of victims, their friends, and uninvolved bystanders is that they insist on the culprit's admitting his guilt, doing penance, and accepting his punishment as just, while the appearance of love, forgiveness, turning over a new leaf is the exception. It cannot be expected, let alone demanded.

Let me give you one example for the application of the Normal-Null concept from the field of your book: a German military doctor who, like me, had been an inmate of Remagen camp, many years later praised the Americans to my face for the splendid job they had done in providing for such masses of PoWs. I couldn't believe my ears till he went on: "They might have let us all starve to death, you know." This was his moral zero-line, and once I kept that in mind, his judgment of American behaviour indeed stopped being merely grotesque.

Much of what you consider incredible behaviour in people and nations, I obviously tend to see as "zero" behaviour. I may any time unite with you and other good people in trying to change the world into something better, but in most instances I would rather not start by railing at others but by acknowledging their given behaviour as understandable and normal and widespread — and wouldn't it be a good idea if they tried something more interesting, exceptional, and morally more ambitious for a change?

The idea that we are our "brother's keeper" and thus do him a favour in criticizing him and removing the scales from his eyes is an intriguing one. But it leads us into deep water. I tend to see moral censure as something by rights reserved to your discourse with yourself. Adverse moral judgment on other people's behaviour I consider as risky morally as it is common. It's so difficult not to interpose yourself between your brother and the ideal you want to lead him to. More often than not you may prevent him from seeing it because you loom so large in front. It is perhaps different with members of a collective unit (nation, family, group, profession, faculty, workplace). They can be thought to share enough of their identity to give the transaction an interior character, analogous to a person battling within himself. That's where the difference between you as a Canadian and member of the war coalition and me a member of the enemy nation lies when we talk of American atrocities. I may with luck do something good by pointing an accusing finger at the Americans, but it is far more likely to have that positive effect if you or a patriotic American does it. For twenty years I kept on hoping that someone else, someone in a better moral position than I, would write "my book." Now, with misgivings, I have written it myself. But how much more good could it work if a Jew or a Pole or a Frenchman had taken up the task!

R.

January 1, 1993

Dear Richard,

Thanks for your letter of September 29. What a letter!

You fascinate me with your ideas of moral normality, and the moral zero on the moral thermometer. And that the moral zero is not just a line but rather a band, within which the judgment of most behaviour would lie most of the time. I like your illustration of the German military doctor who had been at Remagen saying that he thought that "the Americans had done a splendid job of feeding masses of prisoners at Remagen..." And you write, "I couldn't believe my ears till he went on: they might have let us all starve to death, you know." Now the point you take from that is that this was his moral-zero line, which made his grotesque remark at least understandable. And precisely there, I want to say, stop the film; let us look at that frame by frame.

It is now admitted even by defenders of the U.S Army that at Remagen the prisoners were forced to sleep in the mud for months, that they were deprived of food, water, and medicine, that many died. The doctor ignores this crime on the ground that there was not a second. This is his moral zero, I guess.

If all crimes were judged that way, there would be hardly any crime. But there would be far more victims. If judgment came, would the spared prisoners agree to pardon the Americans? What about the relatives of the dead? Would they pity the hangman? It doesn't seem to me tenable, relevant, or interesting for someone to justify one crime by saying he didn't commit a second.

Second, it seems to me that the "doctor's defence" turns on motive. He seems to think that the Americans came to their senses and deliberately spared the other prisoners. One might treat this action as having the quality, or effect, of a confession of guilt, a plea for mercy, an act of expiation. But if so, then one must ask, what was the motive? If to confess, plead, and expiate was not the motive, the "doctor's defence" is invalid.

The U.S. Army got very bad publicity in September 1945. Le Monde *published a devastating article about conditions in French camps, which demonstrated to the Americans that there was a danger that a journalist might expose the conditions in their own camps. There was frantic behind-the-scenes cover-up work going on for weeks, which ended with an agreement with the French to continue shipping prisoners secretly to French hands, while at the same time both Americans and French denied publicly that more prisoners were being sent. Further, the Americans made a token amount of food available to the French, to provide propaganda for the newspapers. The food sent was enough for 10 per cent of the prisoners for under three weeks. Then they starved and died as before.*

On realizing this, one doubts that the American motive at Remagen was to spare the remaining prisoners. I wonder if the good doctor would change his mind once he knew what actually happened. It would probably be much truer to say, "The Americans were worse than they seemed, because they went on killing us although they were afraid of the bad publicity that might result."

So his opinion, I guess, is based on incomplete information. It is an illusion. His moral confusion is caused by illusion.

*Another aspect of his confusion: all the prisoners were punished, some by death, for acts that most had not committed. We know that some of them were innocent of the crimes of the Nazis even in the eyes of the Americans, because they were not even born when they went into captivity. They were born in the camps.** *

Millions of prisoners were convicted and punished without trial, among them your doctor friend. And it appears to me that he has cynically accepted his own guilt, by excusing the Americans of their clear guilt. In effect, then, the whole nation of Germany was convicted, you and your doctor friend among them. It is amazing to many people to discover hypocrisy, but at least it has its roots in a form of self-defence, or ego protection. Now the case of your doctor and of Heising shows us how the Germans have invented an entirely new fault: some of you have buried your innocence in a show of guilt.

Your doctor's words to you are abnormal precisely because they reveal misunderstanding of a reality that they should have been able to grasp, and that was grasped by others in the same situation. His case is exactly like that of Johannes Heising, who saw the American bulldozers drive over his comrades and expunged it from his memory. So I suggest to you that it is dangerous to take the example as showing that doctor's moral null-point. First, it shows his ignorance. The doctor may or may not have

---

* *Many thousands of women, some pregnant, were imprisoned by the Soviets and by the Americans.*

*deliberately ignored reality. Heising certainly did. But any moral judg-
ment of the Americans by either Heising (before the truth struck him) or
the doctor is based on ignorance, and so it is useless to us. Had the doctor
wished to know, had the doctor not feared to know, he could have known.
Hence the power in the parable of the Good Samaritan — not to turn
your face from the difficult, the sad, the ugly.*

*I guess that the doctor's fear is based on his fear of Americans. If in the
1940s or '50s or maybe even the '60s, '70s, '80s, or '90s, he had gone
around saying that "Americans murdered us at Remagen," which is the
exact right word for it, he would have been punished by Americans or
client Germans. Or he feared that he would. I can tell you, I have been
soundly punished here and in the U.S. and in France for saying the same
thing. So if you say that his moral null-point was created in just that
way, I could agree, but only if we can find an answer to the question,
Did the Nazis who murdered Jews because they dreaded Jewish power have
a right to be judged according to this moral null-point?*

*To my mind, you have only once again illustrated one of my central
points about the Germans today, that they/you are morally weak. This
doctor wriggles out of the sad, dangerous duty of telling the truth about
what the Americans did to him at Remagen by inventing this dangerous
lie, that it was okay to kill off a whole bunch of Germans without trial
because not all of them were killed. Sure, and some Jews and Russian
prisoners actually survived Hitler's death camps in Poland, too. Good for
the Germans. The danger to Germans today of their being unable to
defend themselves is clear in the rise of neo-Nazism. You will have to
correct me here if I get some of my facts a little awry because you are so
close to the scene and I am so far away. But as I understand it, the rise of
neo-Nazism is mainly the angry reaction of young Germans to the presence in Germany of many refugee claimants. I have been told that these
claimants are not political refugees at all but people from poor countries
seeking jobs and wealth in Germany. They have been allowed into the
country because of Germany's liberal refugee laws, and, I have been told,
more than 96 per cent of them have been examined by competent Germans
and have been ordered to go home but have evaded the order. This of
course does not excuse the neo-Nazis' violence, but it may help anyone
who, like you and me, wants to find a way out of the mess.*

*The Germans with their very liberal refugee and reparations policies
were trying to show the world that they had learned and reformed. But
they did not get as much moral credit as they probably deserved. This was*

precisely because of their deep continuing guilt. Guilt is a good reaction but a lousy motive.

In other words, if the German authorities had not been impelled by a sense of guilt before the world, all this would have been different. But then, you see, Yitzhak Rabin comes and lectures you on morality, while Israeli soldiers are clubbing kids during the intifada and torturing prisoners in their jails. The British sneer at you, while the Anglo-Irish war that they began and have perpetuated for hundreds of years continues. This is the hypocrisy that we in Canada or the U.S. or Israel or the U.K. or France have, which is based on our moral superiority to you, which continues in existence partly because you, respectable Germans, will not tell the truth about us.

You cravenly and perhaps even with schadenfreude *leave it to the neo-Nazis. You quail. Is that good? Is that a moral zero point or is it a ghastly reminder of your* stunde null, * *so that you all turn to jelly and do whatever you're told by anyone who can remind you of your dreadful guilt. In my view, the guilt must cease to be a motive before Germany can be normal. I am very near to saying that you have no right to question me or my moral judgments, not because you-the-Germans were evil in the 1930s or '40s, but because you are still so cowed by us and by your own sense of guilt. So is that the truth at last? That some of your moral weakness today is my fault? Then my sense of moral righteousness must go. I fall off my high horse and stand in the shitty mud beside you, my friend, my prisoner. But as you know, the prisoner imprisons the guard, as well. I wrote a little poem about that, in France, during* les événements *of 1968.*

The Missing

I was a prisoner of the system
Till I met myself
On exercise one day
At five o'clock.

The guard was like me, familiar, new.
I asked him, "Who are you?"
"You're not supposed to know,"

---

* *Zero hour — the hour of defeat, May, 1945.*

he whispered,
"I am yourself,
I am guarding you."

"We'll have to break together, then," I said.
And when they counted prisoners missing,
There were two.

Well, Richard, I feel, now, that I have met the other.

J.

March 18, 1993

Dear Jim,

I'm tempted to echo you: what a letter! (yours January 1). You make no bones about your wrath. I like that and choose to ignore the humane and poetically intriguing retraction at the end.

There are certain minor or not so minor points I might take you up on, some misunderstandings of what I tried to get across by way of moral philosophy. But I'll leave that for the moment and rather turn to your message loud and clear: what a damn sorry sight we Germans have been presenting to any healthy normal human since 1945! This stands the much more common accusation of a "Second Guilt" — of lacking expiation of the Nazi guilt — on its head.

Well, a majority or pretty large minority of Germans, no longer altogether silent or silenceable, will agree. It's what they have been thinking about official forelock-tugging and pussyfooting Germany for decades. They at least have never lost the normality you appear to miss in today's Germans. All of the CSU (Christian Social Union) grassroots, the refugee societies, and large parts of the CDU (Christian Democratic Union), not to speak of the Far Right, had never any doubt about this. It is true, however, that even most of them let the *Western* Allies off lightly, once the miraculous reconstruction of Germany was on the way. That's probably not mysterious but "normal": nobody in his right senses accuses the whole world, if he can help it. Wronged as he may have been, he will need friends as well as enemies. And for enemies the Eastern bloc did nicely. Beyond that — and building on it: few Western collective crimes were known. You — permit me to say that — have a historical blind spot here, because you were the one to discover some of them in the late 1980s. To the majority of Germans, including most of the inmates of the American and French starvation camps, the thought of having been the victims of an intentional collective death penalty was not seriously to be considered.

So there is still hope for you. Your normal German exists, and if he does not exactly fly to your colours and prefers to remain in his corner, merely keeping his fingers crossed for Jim the Crusader, it is perhaps because — in his normality — he finds that you ask too much of him. You ask him to become a hero in a battle that offers little in the way of reward, is morally not as unconfused as you make it, and may after all turn out to be a lost case from the word go.

Dear Jim, I may or may not be normal, but I definitely have in the course of the past twenty years become impatient with the various kinds of Germans, sometimes even myself included, who look down on normality in others, be they Germans or Americans or Jews. I, like you, consider the German fixation on the German Guilt not normal. But after that our ways part.

Normality for me is something to be used as a point of reference for any judgment and, materially, as the basis from which to undertake any improvement of the world. But it's not something to wax lyrical about. If the Germans individually and, yes, collectively, politically, officially, publicly have chosen to rise above the normal, not letting all-too-normal fellow Germans speak and act for them, I wonder why anyone should dismiss that as bad. After all, half of the world and its media still seem to be wagging their heads over the one-time Nazis making so little progress that way. And shouldn't it be a sobering thought for *any* foreign critics of Germany that from whatever position they start and however their criticisms rule each other out in the end, an admirable Germany seems never to have been in the cards at all?

So while I am in my book busy establishing your idea of normality as the baseline against which German attempts at expiation should be acknowledged as a small but never before observed light in the world of collective national impenitence and smugness, you dismiss us for ever having flouted normality.

It *is* normal to defend yourself, to seek redress for injustice inflicted on you; it is unnatural to turn the other cheek, especially if you are innocent; and if you still choose to do it, you can hardly avoid being called a coward, cringing, etc., because the holier-than-thou have always had a bad press among the normal lot. And no doubt there are dangers lurking that way against which other moral dangers may be harmless — as the history of religions and ideologies testifies. But I don't think, all things considered, that the Germans really have gone too far in this. When not dealing with you I may have harsh words to say about people, inside and outside Germany, who demand of us highly ideal behaviour as something run-of-the-mill — like erecting monuments in remembrance of our country's shame (as if that was a common standard around the world) or welcoming Germany's being cut in two and being robbed of a quarter of its land. If the Germans have come round to doing just that and more, they deserve praise and encouragement, I think. German post-war history, including the moral processing of its lurid past, is not beyond criticism, but some countries could do worse than follow in its steps.

Incidentally, there is a pattern in the history of the German mind that shows us Germans quite prone to fall into the behaviour you describe, a pattern I should certainly hate to see revived. It starts with the assumption that in the concert of nations we Germans are too honest, too good, too just, too disinterested to prosper like the others in their worldly way. Of course other nations indulge that fancy about themselves — the English, for instance, especially when they hit a streak of bad luck — and on the whole it's a harmless delusion and comforting. But the Germans (and again not they alone) have sometimes taken this to such lengths, have considered it so much as God's truth, that it made a head of pernicious self-loathing build up in their national intestines. Poets like Friedrich Gottlieb Klopstock have then been heard to admonish Germania, *Sei nicht allzu gerecht!* (Do not be over-just!). And Germania, resolved at last to be like the English or the French, i.e., normal, all of a sudden stops being just and clubs its neighbours on the head: *Schlagt ihn tot, das Weltgericht/Fragt euch nach den Gründen nicht* (Kill him; the Last Judgment won't ask you for reasons!), as Heinrich von Kleist wrote.

Normality is obviously something dangerous if you try to achieve it with a will. If you approach it from a morally superior position, as is the likeliest case — at least in your imagination — the odds are that in fact you land well below it.

And is it logical for you to demand less German self-accusation and more accusation of the Americans and the French, while demanding that the Americans and the French stop accusing Germany but repent of their own sorry past? Why, if normality is the watchword, should they not go on being normal and refuse to see the mote in their eye? Well, there are the German neo-Nazis now, who, apart from what they *do*, are in fact your normal Germans, which is why initially there was some sympathy for them from thoroughly respectable Germans.

You are very perspicacious on the question of our asylum law. In our *Grundgesetz* (Provisional Constitution of 1949) we certainly were trying to get more moral credit than we were able to pay for. Here indeed guilt feeling and repentance played the fathers of our constitution a nasty trick in 1949. I think anyone familiar with the historical essentials of national justice and law realizes that that tag-on of a sentence to the text of Paragraph 16 of our constitution about "the politically persecuted enjoying the right of asylum" was foolish and untenable. Even if one could distinguish clearly between politically persecuted and economic refugees, how can a nation engage constitutionally, i.e., above its actual national democratic will, to grant asylum to any number of any kind of foreigners? Only a world state with a world court and a world police might just possibly undertake anything of the kind without encouraging trouble. But it's in the German constitution, a constitution hallowed in Germany for good reasons, and instead of this provision being removed on the quiet with a two-thirds majority, it has been made a fantastic bone of contention, most of the contenders not really knowing what is at stake.

In fact, with the loophole of the asylum law (and the Supreme Court forced by its general rulings in other fields to give it precise material substance), no sensible working immigration policy for Germany can be established. I can only hope that the change in the constitution, now in the making between government and opposition, will be what the fierce enemies of the deal call it: a removal of the essence of the German asylum law. As for the young Germans attacking homes of asylum seekers with Molotov cocktails, I am glad that public reaction to them in mass protest marches, candlelight processions, and the like have shown the skinheads that they are not the public heroes they flattered themselves to be. Unfortunately, this general good will has the negative side of fogging the hard political questions that won't go away, skinheads or no skinheads. But that's a subject with too many ramifications to go on about here.

For good measure, I have to make a confession at the end: the military doctor I mentioned in my last letter by way of illustration of what "normal-zero" means as a necessary common ground for moral judgments and who, to my dismay, has come to figure so prominently in your answer, is something of a spectre. Although I did not invent him, I never saw him in the flesh. It was in the summer of 1985, well before *Other Losses* appeared, that in response to the mayor of Remagen's call for a get-together of the former inmates of the PoW camp there, I was walking among the dark stumps of the famous bridge when two ladies, a mother and her daughter, crossed my path. We got to talking; they were also bound for the meeting of the former prisoners, the husband and father, now dead, having been one of them.

I must have suddenly lost the sympathies of the elder lady by an innocent remark I made about the conditions I was forced to live in then, in 1945, for she rather haughtily informed me of what her late husband, the military doctor, used to say on the subject, recalling verbatim the two sentences I passed on to you. You see, there is no reason to refer to him as my friend. In fact, I immediately felt a deep dislike of the type of preacher he seemed to have become after his release. He may even have had to justify some collaboration with the camp authorities in their treatment of us. Anyway, when I wrote my book on normal-zero, I realized that with his second sentence he had somehow changed the character of what he had said in the first. If we had met, we would at least have been able to agree on the facts, while still at odds in their evaluation. Your comment on the doctor's views is impressive, but I don't think you quite fathom his radicalism. He saw nothing criminal in what the Americans did to us. In his mind, even if they had starved us all to death, they would have given us only what we deserved.

R.

April 4, 1993

Dear Richard,

A pastor, Heinz Girwert of Gera, tells us that like Heising, he witnessed terrible events in 1945, and that he suppressed them by a mental mechanism that, I think, he does not fully understand. It appears to be, in sequence: that he saw many men die in the early camps, he suppressed the memory, but then in later camps he saw even more vivid scenes that he could not suppress. He left the camps in that contradictory state of mind, and lived that way with fading memories of the camps, until he read Der Geplante Tod *(Other Losses), when he was forced by persistent uneasy feelings to confront something in himself that would not die, though he had commanded it to. Then by gradually rebuilding his memory, by reestablishing connections long since moribund, he began to remember vivid details that because of the objective evidence of the book he could no longer suppress. So he stands now, believing in the truth of my book and yet wanting to reject it like his own memory. I think you and I can help him out of his painful dilemma, partly by understanding him, and partly by helping him to express himself more clearly.*

Several things about him interest me. One, he is patently honest. He is not trying to curry favour, e.g., by saying, Now I have come to agree with you, dear Mr. Bacque. Another is that he, even more than Heising, appears to me to be truly agonized over all this. And he is even more public. Like nearly all Germans, he has forgotten, because to forget spares him. And now, like some Germans, he begins to remember the German agony. This is fascinating. And he also says that the Germans have forgiven the Americans. That of course excites me: it is the next stage in the debate, and an essential part of our reconciling the various warring parts of this world.

(Later, Toronto April 26)

It is a strange fact that more people are interested in Stalin and Hitler than they are in undoubtedly good men such as Herbert Hoover, or mainly good men such as Martin Niemöller.[10] *Thousands of books have*

---

10 Martin Niemöller, U-Boat Commander in the First World War, became a Lutheran pastor in 1931. After 1933 he preached against Hitler, and was held in two concentration camps from 1937 to 1945.

been written about Stalin and Hitler and their regimes, almost nothing about Hoover and Niemöller. So why does the undoubted truth about people suppressing horror in their own lives not apply on the larger scale? I think the answer to this may have a great deal to do with the personality of individuals, and not so much to do with generalities about human reactions to evil and goodness. And if that is right, the experience of evil shapes the personality in a certain way, whereas in art or history, the experience, being remote, can be taken as dramatic entertainment, and there is certainly drama in Hitler and Stalin. There was drama in both Niemöller and Hoover too, but perhaps the difference is simply scale.

(Later, Toronto, June 1)

The Germans are remembering selectively, which is a normal function of memory. The interesting thing is how the selection is done, and what effect it has on the present day and on the rememberer. We can see some signs of the individual, personal process in the laws of the society. The recent German laws forbidding the defaming of the memory of the dead are on the face of them silly, because if strictly applied they would prevent anyone from defaming Hitler, if such a thing is possible. The laws are based on German guilt exclusively, including the guilt for the Holocaust. Can anyone imagine the German government putting anyone in jail, or expelling a foreign writer, for saying that the Russians did not lose fifty million dead during the war, it was "only" twenty million, or two million. The idea is crazy. Such a person would be asked for the sources of such an amazing revision of history, and if he produced them he would get debate. If he could not he would be dismissed out of hand. Or so we believe. But that is not what has happened to the so-called revisionists.

I have seen on TV film clips of David Irving* addressing audiences in Germany. In one of these speeches, he is saying to a group of young people, some of them skinheads, "No one can tell you that you're war criminals." They are chanting "Sieg Heil, Sieg Heil." Irving, interrupts his prepared speech and looks down at the skinheads and says, "You are mouthing the tired slogans of a criminal past." That bowled me over. Was this the menacing Irving we had been taught to hate and fear? And what was this Englishman doing in Germany teaching young Germans about their past?

---

* David Irving, a British historian, has questioned some aspects of Holocaust history.

Richard, you once told me that you don't remember seeing a single corpse in your cage at Remagen. Yet Heising and his friend were also at Remagen, and they remember not only corpses but bulldozers crushing men under their treads. Did you forget? Did you suppress? Are you afraid of your memories because you are afraid of us? Also at Remagen, one prisoner told me he remembers seeing every morning four or five dead bodies hanging on the wire; Heinrich Koch remembers counting more than eight hundred dead bodies between April 1 and 15. He also remembers them hanging shot on the wire. Did you see that? You write in your report of your time at Remagen and of our subsequent researches that you and the mayor of Remagen find in the stories told by former inmates little or nothing of corpses seen lying about or being dragged away. "The individual sensory memory is generally scant," you wrote.

When I first read that opinion of yours, I was shaken. I thought, Here is a man obviously honest and experienced, quite willing to admit the atrocities I describe, yet unable to remember many, though he was an eyewitness. I simply could not understand that. I knew you were sincere because I had met you, and because you went out of your way to show how such a phenomenon could have occurred, despite your own lack of observation. You counted up the number of corpses there must have been, rationed them out per day per cage and showed that there need only have been two to four a day for four months, and those might not even have been seen dead by other prisoners. This latter fact is correct, as I think I've told you already. For in the American camps, the tent "hospitals" were simply dying grounds, convenient places to collect the dying so that their corpses would not litter up the site and could be more easily transported and hidden. But what never occurred to me has now been revealed in the letters of Heising, his friend Plemper, and Girwert, and even to some extent by the honest Dr. Franken of Freiburg. What happened to most of that experience is that it was forgotten. So perhaps, Richard, you will change your opinion when you see the immense files of evidence we have collected here from voluntary letters from prisoners in Germany chiefly, but including Canada, the U.S.A., the U.K. and France. This may be for you a confrontation with your own memory.

But these things were not simply forgotten: they were eliminated from memory by deliberate suppression. And that this suppression was linked to German guilt was revealed by the good-hearted Pastor Girwert, who writes,

I vow that I have struggled to be honest and that I was aware of the danger of allowing [my] account to veer away from its purpose. And part of my aim was to show that we too had committed crimes and needed a great deal of forgiveness, that, however, crimes had been committed against us and we must grant forgiveness. For that reason I wanted to avoid everything that could lead to the weighing of grief against grief which could set a crime aside as if it hadn't happened. Our own guilt preoccupied me far more than the crimes committed against us so that if that results in a glossing over, then I wanted rather to gloss over what was done to us than what we had done.[11]

Girwert talks about how the Germans forgave the Americans for these things, but how can you forgive a crime if you don't remember it? What do you forgive? This all makes me feel ashamed of the human race. After Hitler, was this the best we could do? Was it even the minimum? Who believes that? I am not afraid of you. I am afraid of lies. I do not want to take them into my soul. I do not want to live by them, and I am living by them as long as I do not admit them. First you have to admit us to the fraternity of guilt by telling the truth. Then you can forgive us.

Only in pain and fear is Girwert retrieving the shards of broken memory like bits of glass from the garbage. With trembling fingers he tries to reassemble the whole, afraid of being cut. Finally, he has most of it back together and it stands before him like a reproach: You did not remember. And it is a reproach because what he does not remember was living human beings, comrades. And now he is guilty for that sin as well. He gave them a second death by refusing to remember them. "If you break faith with us who die, / We shall not sleep though poppies blow / In Flanders fields."

Allow me to quote the poem, from which I took those lines, in full:

---

11 Heinz Girwert, *Allerlei Erinnerungen,* unpublished MS, in the author's possession. Pastor Girwert was in several camps, including Bretzenheim. He lives in Gera.

IN FLANDERS FIELDS

In Flanders fields the poppies blow
Between the crosses row on row
That mark our place; and in the sky
The larks, still bravely singing, fly
Scarce heard among the guns below.

We are the Dead. Short days ago
We lived, felt dawn, saw sunset glow,
Loved and were loved, and now we lie
In Flanders fields.

Take up our quarrel with the foe:
To you from failing hands we throw
The torch: be yours to hold it high.
If ye break faith with us who die,
We shall not sleep though poppies blow
In Flanders fields.

This is perhaps the most famous poem in English to emerge from the
Great War. Since "In Flanders Fields" by its popularity has represented
the sentiments of millions of people who have lived and died in the West
through many decades, it is legitimate to compare it to the sentiments
expressed by Girwert, to see the difference between you and us, and between the Great War and the Second World War. It is clear that the
poem's author, a Canadian soldier named John McCrae, shows none of
the broad, generous sentiments expressed by Girwert. Standing close to
death, McCrae cannot see beyond the quarrel that caused it. To him,
winning and losing are everything. He in effect asks for more death, and
certainly the risk of it, by asking that the living continue "our quarrel."
(Oh, what a petty word for the immense forces that caused the Somme,
Tannenberg, Verdun, the Marne.)

Girwert, who also nearly died, has gone far beyond the poet, to analyze
and describe the forces that drove him and many other Germans, toward
forgiveness of their ill-treatment by the Americans and French. These are
amazingly practical, and were rooted in the impossibility of vengeance,
i.e., that this was the second and last, not the first of the wars. He sums
them up as "... we forgave the Americans so much. How would we have
lived through the forty-year existence of the Deutsche Demokratische Republik

(DDR) without [believing in] an idealistically motivated America?... To hold on to these hopes we all had to play down these bad experiences with the Americans." The undoubted misery of the world is certainly the source of our faith in an unknown heaven. In any case, he calls for forgiveness. He gives it.

Pastor Girwert says that hope was restored to him in St-Paul- d'Eyjeaux, a camp so bad that it was compared to Dachau and Buchenwald by the French writer Jacques Fauvet in Le Monde *in 1945. That camp was to him a war crime, to Girwert a place of hope. And there is another memory blockbuster, for Fauvet now refuses to credit his own writing. His words stand before him in ink on paper, so he cannot deny them, but when I was in Paris in 1991 to talk about my book on the TV program* Apostrophes, *I telephoned him and asked him to meet me to discuss the situation. He refused. He would not uphold his own writing in public. A successful man, former director of* Le Monde, *he had nothing to fear, apparently. Unless public opinion, or the reproaches of the French government conveyed to him by a warning phone call. It is clear that terror must be used to make people suppress their memories.*

So dangerous to the totalitarian regime in the U.S.S.R. was the printed word that they would not allow Aleksander Solzhenitsyn, a war hero flung unjustly into the gulag, to have paper and pencil. So he composed his book in his head. Every day while working he made up new lines, memorized them by repeating them aloud, and gradually grew a whole book in his memory, like a stalactite — drip, drip, drip. This he carried out of the camp in his head. There is a dangerous memory for you. I suggest that the forgetting of Heising, Girwert, and others is similarly willed, but in the opposite direction. It is not just a question of passing by on the other side, or of a natural aversion to horror. Like Solzhenitsyn, these people took their memories of these events out of storage from time to time, removed the horror, i.e., removed the evidence against the Americans, and then put the memory back in place. More and more often they did this, like water polishing away the sharp edges of a stone until it is smooth and round, and different. And I suggest they did this, and perhaps you did as well, because you were all so afraid of us; you knew we had done criminal things, but you were afraid to accuse us. This is not forgiveness, it is impotent fear. And worth no more.

We see today many scary headlines and frightening pictures on TV of the activities of the neo-Nazis and skinheads in Germany. A typical headline was "Dangerous Blooms of the Brown Mire," in the Toronto Globe and Mail, *June 3, 1993. Written by a German, Klaus Bering of*

Deutsche Presse Agentur, and datelined Bonn, the story told of violence against foreigners in Germany. It included statistics: eight foreigners died in Germany in the first five months of 1993 and seventeen died in the whole year 1992. Bering says that about 13 per cent of young Germans surveyed were "determinedly hostile" to foreigners. It is here that the Christian Democratic Union leader, Peter Hintze, finds the "most dangerous blooms of the brown mire," referring to the favourite colour of the Nazis under Hitler. Glorification of violence, war, or racial hatred has reached alarming proportions, according to some German leaders. Some of the fear is based on the popularity of skinhead bands, so even music is brought into it.

These are sad events in a bad trend. One is led to wonder by such stories, Will the Germans never learn? But the same people who deplore what the young Germans are up to, the same Englishmen, Americans, Israelis, Frenchmen, Canadians countenance, use, and defend violence in their own societies, as against Palestinians, Lebanese, Ulstermen and Catholics, black's, religious dissidents. Every lost cause spawns kitschy nostalgia, like the Dixie-lovers in the South, for instance, or the Canadians with a congenital glottal stop who fly the Scottish royal flag over their cottages at Georgian Bay. No one worries that the Dixie flag flew over one of the most repellent regimes known in the modern Western world, which lived off slavery and the slave trade. Loyal to the principles that that flag symbolized, some Dixie-lovers today are still bashing blacks. The way to deal with those criminals is through the police and the courts, not to worry about the return of the Confederacy.

The violence in Germany has so far claimed fewer than eighty lives. This is about the number of charred corpses found in the wreckage of the house where David Koresh died after an American police assault in Waco, Texas. Far more than eight or seventeen lives have been taken by the British and the IRA in the U.K. in the past couple of years, and hundreds of Palestinians and many Israelis are gunned down or beaten or stabbed to death each year. This is a violent world, and the Germans alone are not to blame, nor are the young ones today, by all accounts, any worse or better than the run-of-the-mill wackos and killers whether in uniform or out, in these other countries. And here is a major point, for the law of Germany forbids these acts, and the police regularly drive the young terrorists from the streets, and regularly defend the immigrants and foreign workers. But it is the uniformed police/army in Ireland, in Israel, and in the U.S.A. who regularly shoot the opponents of the regime. It was the government in the U.S.A. that assaulted the religious dissident Koresh, the police who beat Rodney King almost to death in public. It was the Canadian police and Canadian army who faced the aborigines of Oka in a drawn-gun standoff that resulted in one policeman dying and thousands of bullets being fired. And it is both British army and Irish police in Northern Ireland who continue the disastrous feud that began centuries ago and continues hotblooded to this day.

But do we read stories in the Western press deploring militant Zionism, or British imperialism, or American yahoo tactics, with dire warnings about the future? Not so much. Almost not at all. Because these, after all, are "our guys," whereas the Germans are simply not our guys yet. Nor, it seems, will they ever be, except when we need them to prop up a dollar for a while, or strengthen the European economy.

Once when we were talking at Bad Kreuznach, you asked if I thought that the Allies would have used the atomic bomb on a German city. I could hardly believe the question, especially after your experiences in the Rheinwiesenlager. I said yes of course, without a doubt, because I had lived here during the war and I knew the strength of our determination to win, regardless of everything else. You seemed a little surprised at this; I don't know why. Was it because you thought we would be too civilized to use it against Europeans? Against Germans? A European city? What could have prompted that question after Hamburg, Dresden, and the post-war starvation of Germany? More German people died in four years of the Allied occupation than during all the battles on all the fronts. Such a question seems to me invincibly naive. In 1945, would Hitler have used such a bomb against London, New York, or Paris? Would he have invaded neutral countries who had never harmed him, slaughtered millions of women and children in Poland and Russia in order to make the world safer for Germans?

J.

July 17, 1993

Dear Richard,

I want to write an extra letter to you from this cottage at Four Winds Island because here I find peace without conflict. I wrote "peace without conflict," which is a very urban way of putting it: just being here reminds me that what I really mean is tranquillity. Even though here there are gales, thunderstorms, terrific heat, bears, rattlesnakes. This island is paradise, but this paradise has its snakes too, like the other. The foxsnake, five feet long, that can go up a slanting beam up a wall, the rattlesnakes — twenty-four of their rattles are pinned up like trophies on the wall facing me as I write. The question is, What do you do about them? Kill them? The Nazi solution. No one on this island is killing snakes any more. We trap them and move them away, we discourage them, or we learn to live with them, mainly by avoiding them. So we have to learn techniques to deal with the racists in our midst, not by respecting them but by ignoring them, and thus making them impotent. For decades mankind round here has hated and feared and killed the poisonous snakes, and they are still here. As far as anyone can tell, nothing will ever eradicate them. And they are not alone: many people have viewed other creatures here as expendable/eradicable/exterminable — mink, beaver, eagles, bears, moose, bass, pickerel, pike, perch, trout. There is no end to the draw we make on these accounts that seem so vast. And then there are the people not content with paradise. It must be improved. They begin by defining an enemy, which then must be eliminated. This is the myth of progress. Progress meant DDT eliminating birds (along with mosquitoes), meant CFCs to keep us cool (while eliminating ozone). The rule seems to be, the more you improve it, the worse it gets. This is part of what Houston Stewart Chamberlain, Alfred Rosenberg,[12] and Hitler believed: a sort of ethnic paradise would be attained once the minor alien elements were removed. I am afraid that the zealots suffer from an old blindness that will lead to a new cleansing. The signs are all around us. A three-year-old girl I know in Canada said to her mother and father, "I don't like mans," meaning men. Her father, a patient and loving man, explained to her that he was "a man," and that she loved him. A Jewish friend of mine, carrying on against racism in Canada and the "lack of convictions" in Canada's prosecution of alleged war criminals, angrily said, "But if they're guilty they should be charged." A report written by a Canadian lawyer for the Ontario Human Rights Commission said that all charges of racism against

---

12 Houston Stewart Chamberlain, British-born Aryan supremacist who became a German citizen, married the daughter of Richard Wagner and wrote the influential racist *Grundlagen des 19. Jahrhunderts* (Foundations of the 19th Century) 1899. — Alfred Rosenberg, a German politician and journalist from Estonia, inveterate hater of communists and Jews, one of the earliest followers of Hitler, chief ideologue of the Nazi party, who wrote *Der Mythus des XX. Jahrhunderts* (The Myth of the 20th Century), 1930. Hanged at Nuremberg.

named individuals should be believed and acted on a priori until the person charged proved his/her innocence. The minister in charge was reported to have accepted this premise, until attacked publicly in the press. The journalists pointed out, as I did to my Jewish friend, that in our system, people are presumed innocent. The minister and my friend both agreed right away, but they had to be reminded. There was zealotry momentarily hoodwinking basically decent people.

These zealots come armed with the same burning righteousness that the Marxists displayed for seventy-six hideous years, that the Nazis claimed for their brief reign. They said they wanted to eliminate some injustice or some evil, but it usually turned out they meant they wanted to kill anyone different from them. We have lots of criminal law, some based on the principles of righteousness, making pleasures such as marijuana or pain relief drugs such as opium punishable by jail, all in the name of eliminating what is different. It seems that people believe that this has to be part of building a community, but in its extremism, it becomes the zealous and jealous edge. It does not seem to me that it is truly necessary in building a community. In its most extreme form it is also the exact opposite of the urge to community because it expresses only the hatred and rejection that separate people, not the affection, love, tolerance, humour, co-operation, helpfulness — the joys that bind. What is particularly revolting is that you rarely find these zealots — Ian Paisley, Rabbi Meyer Kahane, Michael Kühnen* — preaching anything that cheers diverse humanity on its way. It seems they love to point to the grim combat we must undertake to reach some state of grace hedged with paranoia. Beware the fanatic, especially if he is "one of ours."

The definition of the German as alien, as part of the paranoia defining us "west-of-Aacheners" is very clear from the cover of issue number 42 of Granta *magazine, displaying a swastika emblazoned in suggestive blood colour on a pockmarked concrete wall, above the impatient expletive* KRAUTS! *Inside no lack of self-loathing Germans parade their usual guilts before the English-reading public. To me they are like punch-drunk fighters standing outside a downtown gym preaching the evils of the ring to timid computer-nerds with closed expressions, hurrying by. To the younger people of the West, these Germans are largely irrelevant, but they are made to seem relevant, west-of-Aachen, by such devices as equating the disturbed young criminals of Germany now with the world-menacing Nazis of the 1930s. This brings out bloody fears among our young today: never*

---

* *Top neo-Nazi, died 1991 at the age of 35.*

mind that they live on conquered ground still wet with the blood of murdered tribes of Irish, Scottish, Cherokee, Iroquois, Pawnee, Sioux, Nez Percé, and all the rest. The crucial difference is as always: we are the winners, so history belongs to us, and our history includes no atrocities, until it is too late to matter.

The "KRAUTS!" cover of Granta *succeeds as well because it represents a widespread attitude here: the Germans, the Krauts, are at it again. For all my efforts to get over my dislike of KRAUTS!, I succumbed to my fear of you as I read the magazine. The KRAUTS! who were at it in 1939, who destroyed my father's best friend and wounded or imprisoned members of my family, who murdered the ancestors of my Jewish and French friends, those same KRAUTS! are at it again. Only by remembering the Germans I have slowly, reluctantly, and painfully come to know since 1986 — 1986! — have I become aware that there really are many millions of other Germans who hate all that as much as I, and not just because they suffered, and not just because they suffered retribution, but because they feel the moral revulsion against the past, and against the past-in-the-present that these young skinheads represent. I have met these "good Germans" and I would gladly name them here, but to name them would embarrass them, because I know they feel no pride in simply living decent normal lives. And this is true even though I know that some of them acted very decently during the war, to save the lives of Jewish friends. Normality is not something to praise, we think — until we see the horrifying pictures of masked young skinheads chanting* Sieg Heil *in front of buildings where Turkish women were burned alive. There is no exaggerating the horror of what these young criminals have done, but in order for you to cope with them and for us to cope with you, we both have to understand what drives them.*

According to Granta, *the mother of one fifteen-year-old seized him roughly to prevent him from throwing stones at refugees. She did this, she told reporters later, because she was ashamed. She made him go home, but as soon as he got there, he fled back to his skinhead friends. That woman and the older generation need help and they need it from us, west-of-Aachen.* The confused young man can be saved, because the training he received at home opposes what he is doing. Then why is he doing this? As he says himself, the refugees live off the other Germans, they take jobs away, but also — and here his parents reluctantly agreed with him — he resented the way Germans are treated by other nations. Poles standing on*

---

*   *Aachen, at the western-most point of Germany, is Richard's home.*

ancient German territory seized from Germany after 1945 shouted at them, "Nazis, go home!" The same hatred faced them in Czechoslovakia and Hungary. "The Israelis are saying stuff about Germany again," the son complained. His mother said, "You can't go on blaming us for what happened. I wasn't alive then."

The boy probably does not know anything much about the Second World War except that it happened, or about the Holocaust, except that he thinks it did not happen. He believes it is all a trick by the Jews. It is useless to argue with him because he is not the guilty one. To argue is to try to make him feel a guilt he has already rejected, which even his parents cannot feel personally, because they too were not alive then. The resentment the boy feels is against an influx of refugees that occurred only because of German guilt (as you pointed out, the clause in your constitution guaranteeing the right of asylum was based on war guilt). That clause truly inflicted the sins of the fathers on the second and third generations. But we in the west-of-Aachen have to use our common sense: it is cruel and unjust to make people bear guilt who did not commit crimes. It is time to utter the unutterable word for Germany: forgiveness. It should be simple in 1993: after all, we would be forgiving the innocent.

"Forgiveness!" I can almost hear people all over the West shout. "How can you forgive the butchers of civilians, the people who made aggressive wars against their next-door neighbours twice in twenty-five years? How can you forgive Nazis?"

The process is quite simple. In the west-of-Aachen we forgive the unforgivable all the time. First, you announce the high principles by which your nation lives. You say that you will adhere to these principles to end a certain crime previously widespread. Then, in pursuit of some national interest, you override the principles so you can commit the same crime. In order to preserve the sanctity of the high principles, you cover up that crime. You impede any threat of investigation of the crime. You deny rumours that you committed the crime. You defame the accuser. As the rumours gain credibility, you condemn the victim for creating the evil necessity to commit the crime. Then you minimize and marginalize the crime, saying that although it did not happen, it happened long ago, and in any case, it was the victim's fault, and in order to save other potential victims, you are now announcing the installation of high principles that will prevent the recurrence of the crime.

All this we have already done in order to forgive ourselves for our own crimes, against each other, or aborigines, and so on. The Holocaust deniers of today in Germany are applying to the Germans some of the same self-defensive delusions that we, west-of-Aachen, have long used to salve our own conscience. But of course this is not forgiveness, not even self-forgiveness; it is denial.

I walked to the west end of the island tonight, looking out to the landless horizon where the sun sets in the water now. This view is like the view of an astronaut who sees the round rim of earth through the whole atmosphere, just as one here sees the rim of earth against the universe. I felt the immense sterility of this discussion; I wanted to say as loud as I can to the world, Let there be no limits. Let us not be crippled by great visions, let us live day to day, person to person. Every small garden grows from that infinite sunfilled sky.

J.

July 21, 1993

Dear Jim,

I did not answer your letter of July 4, as I was to see you in person, thanks to your kind invitation to Toronto. Now I am back, my mind full of your wonderful country, your wonderful hospitality, and the endless talks about what we try to understand and perhaps help others understand. But has it become easier for me to answer your letter? I wonder.

Let me first grab the nettle of the questions you fire at me personally, and don't think that I resent that. I'm only afraid that my answers will still disappoint you.

You steadfastly assume that while in the camps I saw people dead and dying. You remain convinced I must have. Why then, you ask, don't I remember? You say you know that I am not a liar, so you think it must be due to something else. Suppression seems the obvious answer. And why suppression? Because, you say, we feared the Americans, the victors.

You ask me point-blank, Richard, were you afraid of us?

The answer is a flat no. I for one did not fear the Americans, I loathed them. And of course even without heaps of corpses around me, there was plenty to loathe them for. It boggled my mind the way they treated us. Who would have thought that possible? Who would ever believe us if we got the chance to tell? The Russians, yes — everyone knew what the Russians were capable of. But the Americans?

That's why I documented the daily rations in my diary, for otherwise I might not credit my own memory once it was all over. And, it's true, there was constant *rumour* of prisoners falling ill and probably dying by the dozens — which I had no difficulty believing vis-à-vis the brinkmanship I exercised night after night to prevent me from being one of them. I believed it the more readily, as it had the psychologically well-known effect of raising my spirits: in spite of everything, these bastards were not succeeding in doing *me* in. Not so far. Wasn't that something to be modestly proud of? Also, I had the psychological advantage of not having chosen imprisonment. I had in fact tried to avoid it till the only alternative was being dead the next minute. Logically, I could not feel quite the same resentment as those around me who had dreamed of American prison camps as a decent transit to peace and security. Bewildered though I, too, was by what was done to us, the focus of my mind was not really on the perpetrators — they were just part of the inscrutable background to all the surprises war had a habit of springing on you as you turned another of its corners.

The question foremost in my boyish mind, ever since I was called on to contribute to my country's war effort, had been, How will I cope? How well will I bear myself even in this? "This" meant the danger every night at the age of sixteen of the air raids on Cologne, thirty-six feet up on top of a wooden anti-aircraft tower; the humiliating chicanery in the Reichsarbeitsdienst (Compulsory Labour Service) in 1944; at seventeen, the encounter with American tanks; at eighteen, shooting them dead, eye-to-eye, in their open armoured vehicles with our bazookas or machine guns; surrendering to the Americans on April 11th, 1945; and now: Remagen (from April 24th to May 11th).

But come to think of it, not even at Remagen was one day like the next, and anything I say in order to sum up an experience of months can only be partly true. That soldiers, not policemen, not gangsters, but soldiers, essentially in the same boots as ours, who might easily have been at our mercy as we now were at theirs — that *soldiers* should sink so low as to beat other soldiers walking obediently in double line into Remagen camp, with wooden clubs, beating them into formation, obviously under higher orders, as if driving slaves or cattle — that, to me, was the most inexcusable thing of all. After that anything might happen.

No, Jim, I had no feelings of guilt, neither personal nor national — nothing along that line to help me understand what they were doing to us. Girwert remembers differently. He seems to have had knowledge of German crimes, perhaps of things he might reproach himself for. Or was he just the more sensitive, more Christian type? Significantly he, like Heising, became a clergyman later. But I dare say, feelings of guilt were damn rare among prisoners in those days, partly for the reason that so many German soldiers had never consciously committed crimes or had seen them committed, partly because they were "normal" humans tending to think well of themselves and their mates (and definitely incapable of self-criticism while being exposed to their own extermination), and partly because they were Nazis who had their own ideas about what was a crime and what was not. As for me, defeat was what I had to come to terms with emotionally. We had got into a fight, and in spite of all our bravery, we had again been beaten and were now being humiliated by rubber-soled gangsters. As so often in history, the gods had been on the side of the undeserving and evil had once again been allowed to triumph. That this feeling was really mine then I infer from the first two lines of one of the poems I scribbled into my little diary, which survived.

Die Nacht hat einen Spaten
und gräbt der Sonne ein Grab,
in Feindeshand bin ich geraten,
nicht Dach noch Bett ich hab'.

Was andre wie's Leben besitzen,
das darf ich von ferne schau'n,
und geh ich, dann lachen die Spitzen
höhnisch vom Stachelzaun.

Ich lache auch zu Stunden,
doch lache ich nicht froh,
das kommt von den tiefen Wunden,
und diese bluten so.

Und keine einzge Träne,
löst mir im Auge sich,
mein Lachen trennt nur die Zähne,
halb Narr, halb Bettler ich.

Wenn doch den Tod ich fände
dann käm' ich in stille Hut,
so wüsst ich doch das Ende,
und also wär es gut.

The night, it has a spade
and digs the sun a grave.
In hostile hands I've fallen,
nor roof nor bed have I.

The life that others have,
I see only from afar,
moving, I meet the barbs
that prick me on the wire.

I sometimes laugh like others
but never out of joy,
because of the wounds within
that bleed so terribly.

But not a single tear will
escape my weary eye,
my laugh just parts my lips,
half fool, half beggar I.

If only I could die,
in perfect peace I'd lie,
where suffering's done at last,
and all accounts are closed.

It is true, I have known quite a lot of Germans in my life who
would never stick out their necks, who would keep mum rather than
risk any unpleasantness — under Hitler, after Hitler, in school, in
the army, on the job. It was natural to them, an inborn survival

instinct, I guess. To my unbelieving ear, even long after the war, Germans seemed to live in an irrational fear of revenge by the Americans, should they come out with something detrimental to Yankee reputation. I used to know a pharmacist, older than I, who had been in Bolbec PoW camp before my time and over the counter once hinted at horrible things he had witnessed there. I told him what memories I had of the place. It had had makeshift tents (though without any kind of floor or bedding). There had also been hot soup twice a day, but with so few calories that I had the shock of my life when one warm summer day I took off my Wehrmacht rags and found that after three months in American custody the flesh had literally vanished from my body and that I could join the thumb and middle finger of one hand around my thigh. On another day I had watched a prisoner being punished by being forced to stand bare-headed on a post in the burning sun, at last collapsing and crashing to the ground — to his death, as rumour had it. Yet my pharmacist dried up and played for time when I asked him to tell me more, threatening to take "these old stories" down. Every time I mentioned the subject — this was in the early 1980s! — his look became more hunted, and I gave up.

But I myself was not afraid, never, of anyone, at any time of my life, not, that is, till that inborn impudence of mine got me into a real corner of physical danger. Then I might cave in — or not, as the case might be. No, fear cannot explain suppression in me, if suppression there was. In the face of so much of my life I've forgotten or remember only dimly, I'd welcome any bit of it, good or bad, favourable or unfavourable, to make its appearance through a chink in my aging brain. Till then, I have no choice but to stand by my memory for what it is worth.

If in 1945 I did not see what I might have seen and others obviously did, the explanation, apart from that by accident it just did not happen where I was, may lie in my particular way of coping with starvation and mud and cold. I can indeed see Richard Matthias Müller, eighteen, shutting himself off as best he was able from the outside world, reducing his motions, his vision, his feelings, withdrawing into his motorcyclist's greatcoat to a world of dreams and poems.

I like your little gem of psychological insight: of good Germans taking their camp memories and polishing them till there are no rough edges left that would tell against the Americans. I can see Girwert and Heising and my military doctor and many other politically and morally sensitive or, for that matter, plain down-to-earth and forward-looking Germans do it, especially years and decades after the event. But out of fear? My pharmacist refused to speak out of fear, all right, but for all I know he was not one to polish.

Girwert's moving statement, that he "wanted rather to gloss over what was done to us than what we had done" points in the direction of a scrupulous, refined conscience, which sees the mote in its own eye rather than the mote (or beam) in the eye of the other. If there was fear at the bottom of some German's polishing, it was probably the much more subtle fear of deviating from some mainstream German opinion. Some may have polished their camp memories in order to make them acceptable to the fold of virtuous Christians or anti-fascists, while others may have done the same in order to conform to a general pro-American trend in Germany from '48 onward. Deviation from the prejudices of a group one belongs to or cares for is a serious business, as I don't need to tell *you*. Unless one has turned it into a way of life (some indeed seem to thrive on it) or has managed to get one's maverick status good-humouredly accepted by the group, be it large or small, one will risk one's health through social censure and isolation. But then most German PoWs needed little persuasion one way or another to forget what nobody seemed keen to hear. The enormous strain and horror of almost six years of war, and more years of camps afterwards, had naturally left a desire to relax, to enjoy life again, to build some better future, instead of wasting even more precious years licking old wounds.

My case was somewhat special in two ways, yet leading to the same result. For one, the tale of woe I could tell did not include American or French homicide — I must insist on that. And second, after Remagen and Bolbec, I got into an American camp where, except from being illegally held in custody for an undefined period (till November 1946, as it turned out), I was fairly well off and given the chance to open my eyes and see and read and infer what the democratic West had to offer to thinking Germans, even to a German like me still perversely proud of Germany.

But while I found much to admire in the American way of life, from the writings of C. A. Beard[13] down to the disobedient war

13 Charles A. Beard, *The Republic*, The Viking Press; New York, 1943.
14 Bill Mauldin, *Up Front*. Henry Holt NY 1945. - *Stars and Stripes*: Newspaper of the US Army.

cartoons by Bill Mauldin in the *Stars and Stripes*,[14] I still felt and resented the weight of Western smugness around us, all the anti-German falsehoods, historical distortions, and arrogant prejudices in the American press and in the occasional German *Neue Zeitung*'s special edition for prisoners of war, intended to de-Nazify and re-educate us. I had been shown *Life*'s photo report of the Germans of Weimar being driven through Buchenwald concentration camp at gunpoint to take note at last. But did these things, deeply disturbing as they were to me, give anybody the right to tell lies about the Germans and forbid the Germans to answer back? I had in general been an admirer of the Führer, but that had never prevented me from seeing and criticizing what to my lights were falsehoods, stupidity, and patent lies in Nazi Germany. I could not and I would not change my critical scepticism to appease a new bunch of dictators keeping me behind barbed wire for no reason I could see and feeding me with stupid, self-indulgent propaganda.

My impression that Germany, and myself as a German, was not going to get a chance of a fair hearing, the feeling that we were sure of being howled down by a fanatical VE Day mob every time we should raise our voices in self-defence, stopped only just short of paranoia.

I still have in my possession a text I wrote in camp Philip Morris, of course in German and camouflaged as a quotation.

> If this were a fight! Grateful would I be if I were allowed to defend myself against superior forces, even if a thousand strong. But, lo! Here I stand as in the middle of a muddy pool whose foul and stinking waters reach between my nose and my mouth. I may breathe, I may live, but what if I dare open my mouth!
>
> Yet I feel it building up in me, feel how the urge to speak, to cry out, to defend myself against lies and defamation grows. Soon it will have reached its mark and there will be no stopping it. Then my mouth will open, and all that the world is going to hear before the cesspool chokes me will, at most, be a scream.

When at last I could no longer bear not to "open my mouth" it led to the mad venture of writing a long letter to one of the American officers at my workplace, Camp Philip Morris, Block 2 Supply.

I was not "howled down," I just got no answer, not from this young warrant officer who I had imagined would be shaken by the force of my arguments. Instead, months later, I found I had offended some GI guard who was watching over our disgruntled "detail," which was removing rusty old nails from the remnants of the once-proud camp Philip Morris. Without changing his squatting position with the rifle over his knees, he dropped the hint that someone hoping to be released soon might be turned over to the French instead. "And by the way," he added, "if I were you, I wouldn't write letters to American officers."

I'd give the world for a look at the message I had then felt compelled to send to my American custodians — for an insight, that is, into my 1946 mind.

But to the heart of your letter, to the point where your thoughts dive deep indeed and where I tremble to follow. You hear the pastor say that we Germans "forgave" the Americans; and knowing you and seeing you in my mind's eye, I think you can hardly rein in your temper at this. How can these Germans, you fume, forgive something they have forgotten and the Americans for their part do not dream of asking forgiveness for?

Your letter tells me that you are in no doubt about the moral and logical order of things: first, there is the duty of the Germans — if duty can be called what should be natural in a human being — to register, honour, and mourn the deaths and sufferings of their fellow countrymen. Second, it would be the duty of the Americans and the French or the Allied nations as a whole to look into and face the truth of crimes committed by or in the name of their alliance, and welcome whatever help outsiders, including Germans, should provide toward that end. Germans then should not spare Americans and Frenchmen those accusations that they, the Germans, are primarily able and entitled to raise. Evidence of American and French admittance of guilt provided, Germany may then proceed to the act of forgiving.

And what about German guilt, the guilt figuring so prominently in the German mind nowadays that you think it has come to warp our whole moral, political, and legal reaction system? Well, if I understand you right, after Germany has repented and made amends and the Americans and the French in turn have looked into their own cupboards, they should then forgive the Germans, at least the innocent ones, because, as you say, guilt can never be worked off by the guilty nation alone. If it is not to poison the lives of all parties concerned, it must be forgiven. In fact, you feel shame that on the part of the Allies forgiveness has not been offered yet.

Dear Jim, what you write makes absolute sense to me. I couldn't agree more.

Why then my trepidation?

Well, everyone may have a picture in his mind of what the world should look like. Anyone, including Germans, may dream. And some Germans may with a kind of horror imagine what the consequences may be if German dreams remain for too long just that.

And yet: to turn a German's dream, no matter how innocent it may be in itself, into demands and, if not fulfilled, accusations, addressed at the victims of German aggression and crimes, i.e., at Poles, at Czechs, at Dutchmen, at Americans or Canadians, at *Jews* is a different matter, even two generations after the war.

A matter of *courage*! I hear you say, a matter of normal national courage. And a matter of duty. You Germans, I hear you say, simply have the duty to make the Americans see the truth and to stop them defending their false innocence with lies. "And don't think so much of what they or the Jews or anybody else will say in their righteous indignation. German reputation is ruined anyway, and your stance in the international sympathy rating scale is hopeless — don't fool yourselves about that. So you might as well be just normal and courageous. That, in the end, may pay better dividends than trying to be everybody's darling at the expense of truth (and James Bacque)."

I listen. I ponder what you say, and what I hear you say in my mind. Basically we are as near as two people starting from opposite national and biographical positions can probably be.

And yet something warns me not to let me be advised by you.

One day, when I was young, in the days of Hitler, I noticed that among the prose and verse I had been writing there was not a single sentence that showed any enthusiasm for the things then high on the patriotic agenda. All evidence of loyalty to the regime would be found missing, should the Gestapo get the idea of raiding my desk. (Raids by the secret police and how I would defend myself success-fully before the *Volksgerichtshof* (People's Court — a Nazi implanta-tion into the judicial system) were favourite fantasies of mine.) It was the week of the fall of Stalingrad [January 1943], and I decided to conform to what a glorious national future would expect of a young writer to have written in the days of Hitler's Great War. I entered in my diary some solemn sentences about the heroic fight in the East and of confidence in a final German victory by drawing a parallel between Stalingrad and Thermopylae (without knowing that Hermann Goering had got the same idea).

Then, after the war, back from camp Philip Morris, I reread the things I had written during the Nazi years and was pleased to find that I could stand by everything I had written, that at least it was a true reflection of my former self. But then I came to this entry, and my blood pressure shot up. How would I have liked to undo this! Not because it compromised me, now the times and myself had changed — after all, I *had* been a Nazi and was not going to deny it — but because this proof was a fake. I had written not from my true self but in an attempt to be somebody else. I had not lied — I believed what I wrote. But in writing it I had turned myself into a propagandist and thus betrayed my gift as a writer. On that day I swore that whatever wrong or foolish thing I might say or write in the future, it would at least be my own thing, not dictated by the zeitgeist, or to please nice people or good friends.

Well, that's still with me. And there is a more general side to this. Truth is one thing, but to proclaim it, another. What you say should be the truth, but it should also be the time and the place for it, and you the right person to lend it words. If I should choose to tell someone out of the blue that it's now half-past seven, I would be telling the truth. And yet he might doubt my sanity, there being no apparent reason why I said it.

Thus if the German government should decide to embrace your position as stated in *Other Losses*, the American government would be sure to wonder what the hell they were up to, suddenly accusing them at this point in time of having deliberately mistreated German prisoners of war and caused 700,000 of them to die. Are they playing the Russian card? (That's unlikely now that the Russians have nothing to offer them.) Or do they want to obscure their poor economic track record and put their electors off the scent? As a plausible answer is not easy to find, German governments prefer not to embrace and proclaim the truth of *Other Losses* (or be seen supporting James Bacque proclaiming it).

And that applies to the majority of Germans. What credible answer can they give as to why they would be bringing forth accusations against the French and the Americans for Remagen, Bretzen-heim, and the rest?

Perhaps the most natural, and consequently most credible, an-swer would be that by this time the Germans are simply sick of being the only ones on the receiving end of such accusations — that we wouldn't at all mind the Americans and the French, but especially the Americans, the main preachers in the field, to share some of the burden we have had to shoulder.

But this is an inadmissible motive, discrediting the whole thing right away. *Aufrechnen von Schuld* (weighing of guilt against guilt) is the last thing the Germans would be caught at. What else, then? Historians might just get away with the assertion that they are only after truth, routinely revising errors in the records of world history; but even they, if German, would have to take special precaution against being suspected of more sinister motives.

And take me. What will I say when asked about my motives for supporting James Bacque? Tell of the dream we appear to have in common? The telling of dreams may be the very thing to undo them. But you are one of the victims, you will say. Okay. But can I play the victim's part convincingly, from the heart? Looking into myself, I don't think I can. And even if I could, could I believe in the success of my campaign for the truth of *Other Losses*? And wouldn't you have to forgive me for shunning a lost cause, if I couldn't?

As Ernst Jünger, much-maligned, much-praised German writer and soldier, decorated with the highest German order in the Great War, said in his diary of March 26, 1981, "Truth and Effect are only accidentally married at a particular historical juncture. Truth can remain without effect, or even call forth its opposite. Those are Golden Ages when Truth and Effect are in accordance." Are we on the threshold of a Golden Age — we, that is, Germany and the world?

The best and strongest motive for me to engage myself in this matter of *Other Losses* is exasperation and fury at the way you, your book, and your witnesses are being treated in America and France. The governments, the press, the historians of these countries don't like what you have to say, and they may perhaps count on the major-ity of their peoples to feel the same. For, after all, you ask them to acknowledge something that is hurtful to their collective pride, some-thing hard to swallow. I can sympathize with their aversion because it is so "normal." However, not liking what James Bacque writes is one thing, but trying to kill it by slander, by ridicule, by lies, by bullying, by suppression of evidence, by academic filibustering is something quite different. I should think it everybody's duty to prevent *that* from becoming normal.

And yet, wherever ideology and fanaticism reign supreme, even that is normal. To stamp out by any means available what does not conform to the reigning overall "truth" is considered not only normal in these countries but highly virtuous. That's true of all fascist and communist states; it should not be true of countries with living democratic and liberal traditions.

But, alas, Hitler's mortal challenge of half the world between 1939 and 1945 led also, tragically, to an undermining of Western liberal bastions, such as they were. At least in one respect the West became just as fanatically ideological as any fascist or communist country: in its anti-Germanism. Anything that confirmed Germany's well-earned reputation as a monster — should that anything be truth, half-truth, error, lie, or slander — was welcomed and propagated by all means available, and anything that might show Germany in a favourable light and her opponents in an unfavourable one was to be frowned on, ridiculed, thundered against, suppressed, or simply forbidden. While other run-of-the-mill anti-X-isms have been effectively ostracised by civilized societies in the past forty years or so, anti-Germanism in the guise of anti-Nazism is having an eternal field day among the virtuous of the world.

That's what you are essentially up against, dear Jim, and you know it.

But that's nothing compared with the difficulties a German fighting the same cause will encounter, while your credentials as a Canadian and erstwhile German-hater allow you to feel and act as a veritable St. George rescuing truth from the fangs of prejudice and vested interest. A German assisting you is ostensibly nothing but an unredeemed old Nazi, and may to his horror feel like one.

July 28

This letter is now long enough to be mailed, but I understand you are away on Four Winds Island for another ten days, which means I might as well carry on for a couple of pages, as you won't be able to answer for a while yet. (Lucky you, to be marooned on that enchanted island. How well I remember the day you introduced us to it!)

You mention certain German laws and shake your head in disbe-
lief. Like our now world-famous constitutional asylum law, these
laws seem to prove that Germany in attempting to right the wrongs
of its Nazi past has somehow gone over the top. How, you ask, can a
country in its right senses make it punishable by law "to defame the
dead," meaning that you will go to prison if you defame millions of
Jews by saying that they were not murdered. What about Hitler, you
say. He is dead, and would I not be allowed to say anything deroga-
tory about him in Germany?

Well, as usual in law, things are more complicated than appears
in newspapers. For one thing, the law against defamation
(*Verunglimpfung*) was introduced under the Nazis. It refers to public
statements about a dead person, which are contrary to fact and
uttered with the intent to slander. This law wouldn't help Hitler, as
only near relatives are entitled to appeal to it. But that apart, why
should not even a Hitler be protected from that kind of thing?

The law as it now stands has indeed a particular edge with regard
to Jews in so far as a clause has been added to the effect that in the
case of Nazi victims, public prosecution is also admissible. It simply
seemed grotesque that the efficiency of the Nazi murder machine,
wiping out any near relatives, should profit the defenders of Nazism.

Things become even more complicated by the fact that this law is
not the one sometimes referred to as the law against the "Auschwitz
lie." This law, as I found out to my own astonishment, is conspicuous by its non-existence (in a formal sense). Its introduction into
German law was debated for five years, under Helmut Schmidt and
under Helmut Kohl, and finally rejected.[15]

Instead, an older law against "insulting someone by making insulting remarks about a dead relative" ("insult" being applicable
only to the living) was changed, so that in the case of making insulting remarks about victims of Nazi genocide, every living member of
that "genus" (i.e., nation) could stand as an insulted "relative." As
this law says nothing about what constitutes an insult in such cases,
it can be applied with discretion and flexibility, every case having to
be judged on its particular merits. Publicly denying the death of
millions of Jews in Nazi camps may in fact not suffice. Conviction

---

15 This was the state of things when this letter was written. Meanwhile a formal
law has been passed making the Auschwitz lie as such punishable. It has
been used to put people in jail.

will depend on the intention, the situation, the person who says it, etc. If, however, the culprit has said or written, They were not murdered, but what a pity they weren't, he'll probably be in for it.

The skinheads and neo-Nazis I think I'll leave for another letter. But for good measure I ought to take you up on the "Atom Bomb on Germany." I don't remember asking you whether the Allies would have dropped A-bombs on Germany, but I imagine I wanted to tease out some racist element in America using Japs as guinea pigs for the miracle weapon. You think it's a foregone conclusion that the Allies would also have A-bombed Germany without compunction, just as Hitler would have wiped out Paris or New York. But the question is, Would they have done it when, as I contend in the case of Japan, it was really not much more than the irresistible fun of trying out and showing off a new and God-like weapon, probably meant to impress the whole world, especially the Russians, as much as the Japanese? (Incredible as it may appear to you, I can imagine quite a few German generals sabotaging Hitler's command to wipe out Paris. In fact Gen. Dietrich von Choltitz did just that — saved the capital of France, ignoring Hitler's command).

But let me finish before more silly speculations get past my control unit.

R.

August 13, 1993

Dear Richard,

I am convinced now. I no longer think that you are suppressing images of horrors at Remagen. I believe your explanation must be correct, that you simply shrank into your wonderful coat, which saved your life. Think of great playwrights, who condense huge events into symbols as powerful as that coat of yours.

I was struck by your casual remarks about how you were impressed by American books like Charles A. Beard's and Bill Mauldin's war cartoons. Was that the beginning of a new orientation with you? Or what was it that turned you from a Hitler Youth into a democrat? Would you care to tell me?

Here and there you say things that show me there is something like a generation gap between us, although we are only a couple of years apart in age. I guess this is because you fought, and were captured, and suffered, and almost died, whereas I went to school, put pins in maps, read about war, played soldier with a German army First World War souvenir helmet, and took relief parcels to the Red Cross and the post office, and missed my father and sister and brothers away at the war. It is very odd to think that you and I hated each other without knowing each other.

Your experience has made you ashamed and sad, but never untruthful, though many Germans before and even now have hoped to evade responsibility for the past. Mine, I guess, made me very demanding of our victory: I want, I desperately need, our Victory to mean and to have meant something. What? To save Europe, I suppose, to bring to life democracy, freedom, civility, truth, to teach more people to wear life with a smile. And what I see now is so different that sometimes I feel like hanging my head in shame like a German.

You know my family is French in origin, and that I long lived in France. When I came out of the French army archives at Vincennes the first time, having discovered some of what they did to the surrendered Germans in 1945, I was so angry that I threw my beret on the ground and stomped on it. (But then my family is also Scots, so I picked it up.)

I have a vicarious, and you a direct, experience of war, so you are cautious where I am bold. That's why I respect your decision not to take my advice to protest more against the crimes of the Allies. By the way, don't imagine I ever felt I needed to seduce you to my side of the argument about Other Losses *because I need more supporters in Germany. I was confused at first by the huge difference between your honestly reported experience and that of so many others, so I wanted to chase down the reason, which we have now done. I like you as you are, and for purposes of this book and our friendship, I need you as you are, independent. About, I should think, as we in the West need Germany now, independent and amiable.*

You say, "The gods were on the side of the undeserving, as so often." Which is the opposite of the way people in the English-speaking countries usually feel. We are optimistic, problem solving, we believe in "the future" and our own good fortune. Can this be because we have won all our wars and spread our empire all over the earth? Is there a continent we have left uninvaded? Any country we did not invade was probably undesirable. The British told God to Save the King, and Send Him Victorious, Happy and Glorious; the Yankees ordered God to Bless America. And Canadians ask God to Keep Our Land Glorious and Free — all these could only have been thought or sung by an English-speaking person who expected that God would obey. And Who did obey. There, I guess, is some of my problem about our behaviour. I did not realize in 1943 when I was hugging my sister goodbye in her Royal Canadian Air Force uniform in Union Station that the crusade she was on had been partly sullied by our long, empire-building, profit-making venture. Our virtue had a bottom line, which accounts for some of what we did to you. It is why we did not care much about our victims.

Your saying that most German soldiers felt no guilt partly because they were Nazis astounds me. I had thought most were not Nazis. Or do you mean that they accepted the identification of Germany and the Nazi Party as long as you were winning the war? And hence to lose is only to lose, not to feel guilty, because you were fighting for a cause, just as we were?

The lack of German zivilcourage (a phrase we don't have in English) vis-à-vis the occupying Americans seems to me not irrational at all. Even Konrad Adenauer feared them and refused to speak out against the crimes that he had witnessed in the Rheinwiesenlager. Willy Brandt also feared to tell the truth, or even to let others tell it. With such pusillanimous leaders, what could ordinary Germans do? But can you be right about why Girwert and Heising polished their memories, removing the horrors? Your explanation is not all-inclusive: it was not simply that lacking zivilcourage, they adhered to a norm. You fail to explain how the norm was established. And I suggest it was established by millions of individual decisions taken by scared Germans not to denounce the American crimes for fear of the American conquerors. For many Germans, "good behaviour" is guaranteed by fear of the conqueror, not by fear of repeating your mistakes of the past. The Nazis rise as we depart. There is little remorse in your guilt; there is much fear.

The American reaction to your critical letter in Camp Philip Morris shows that the German civilians were right to fear the consequences of denouncing American crimes. Still, it might have gone worse for you; they might have sent you to the French right away. Perhaps they feared to lose your precious translating skills?

In any case, there soon came to Germany a much better American policy, under leaders who represented their best values, Hoover, Truman, and Gen. Mark Clark. Maybe even Lucius Clay, to some extent.

Your image of the cesspool and the scream made me think of Edvard Munch and Bertolt Brecht and Samuel Beckett, all white male Europeans. Such an agonizing image could not possibly come from a white male North American.

You tremble to follow my thoughts re Germany's reaction, and you observe that I have no doubts re the moral and logical order of things. True, I don't. But I do not agree that the prime duty of the Germans is to mourn the deaths of their fellow countrymen. Rather, to mourn the deaths of all those you murdered on the field, in their homes, in your camps, along with mourning your own soldiers and civilians. The dead have no citizenship. Then, without hypocrisy and by showing in peace the courage you showed in battle, you could tell the truth about us. Under Brandt and Adenauer, Germany was a nation of cowards and liars. Is it still? If reasonable people will not tell the truth, is it because they hope the neo-Nazis will? I suspect there are many Germans like that. We agree that you have nothing to lose internationally, so you might as well speak out. There is truth in that, as you can see from the cover of Granta that I mentioned in my last letter and a copy of which I enclose. Don't let the neo-Nazis take over the truth.

But no, I have to admit that I cannot yet live up to the ideal of forgiveness that I advocated in my last letter. I feel little shame that we are not forgiving Germany. I don't really want to forgive Germany, not yet. It involves too much rethinking of all my old attitudes. Nor do I see how I could forgive the cruel stupidity of Hitler: think of Operation Barbarossa and the extermination of the peoples of the East, and now look at Germany, rich, powerful, extending help to the East, taking in refugees. I don't see how I could ever forgive German arrogance, which was close to the root, if not the root, of the atrocities. But I do feel shame at the wrongs we committed against you after the war, which harmed us as well as you.

We really need to forgive each other, I guess. That is where we would have to start. And that would begin with a truthful rewriting of history. A. J. P. Taylor, Richard Overy, Nikolai Tolstoy and Alfred de Zayas have made a beginning, along with some others (I would like to be included), but no German or Frenchman. Lies abound, hate prevails.

You make much of the difference between truth and the effect of proclaiming it. I don't doubt that there are two cases, but I cannot accept your argument. We are still enslaved by the hatreds of that war. It seems sometimes to be still happening on the other side of the hill. How to be free of it? Jesus Christ said the truth shall make you free. But he did not promise that the truth is free. You have to free the truth first. And that costs. Are you afraid of that cost, for Germany?

But still, maybe Christ would also say fear of the truth is a prison cell.

You suggest that there might be a natural motive for you Germans to denounce our crimes. You might say, We are sick of being the only ones who are guilty. Get down here with us. But we would have to agree to get down beside you. And why should we? To show we feel sorry for you? That would be false pity, a wallowing in emotion, a sentimentality that has the same roots as nationalism. That leads nowhere. My answer to you is, Why should we share your burden? Only because we forgive you. But forgiveness is exactly like truth. It costs, but it frees you, in this case from hatred. So we would have to be truthful and forgiving. In other words, first we become perfect, then we will be happy. Ahem.

But there is some hope; we do go, little step by little step, erringly toward that perfection. I hope you and I are on that path, and not simply following again the corpsy road to utopia. You say you want to defend Other Losses *because of the cruel slanders and lies levelled against me and the subject in the West. But just remember how much I have been defended and helped, by Elisabeth Bacque, Jessica D., Dr. Ernest F. Fisher, Dr. Anthony Miller, by Prof. Peter Hoffmann, Julian Barnes, Richard Overy, Pierre van den Berghe, by Stephen Ambrose himself (before his conversion), by Paul Boytinck, Alfred de Zayas, and many, many others. Including you! Without this support, I would have cracked long ago. The amazing thing is that not a single academic or writer in France, and only one in Germany, Karl-Heinz Jansen in* Die Zeit, *has spoken out in favour of the obvious truth in the book. On the contrary, official opinion in both countries, emanating from academe, the press, and government, has libelled me mercilessly and denigrated the research. So the place to start is Germany, I think, difficult though it may be. But it is not necessary for you to do it. The figures from the Soviet archives are going to silence even the governmental critics and force some embarrassing admissions from former opponents of the truth.*

As for this debate sometimes making you feel like a Nazi again, I am appalled. How horrible. Were you the one with the spray can in the Allied war cemetery the other night in Nijmegen defiling Canadian war graves with swastikas? Of course not. But that is what the little Nazis did, eh? I am sorry you have had even a frisson of that, but then I think back to the days when I was young and ran half a mile along a portage in Algonquin Park with a ninety-pound canoe on my head because I felt so good, strong, joyful, and young. For me to remember that no more means I could do it again than I could wish upon the Ruhr cities even the smallest part of what I grimly wished upon you long ago. So your Nazi frisson is inevitable but without consequence today. It is the feeling in the amputee's phantom stump.

But another part of the stump is itching too, the law. Thanks for the word on the origins of the anti-defamation law. I had no idea the Nazis put it in, and with good reason too. However, David Irving was convicted under a different section, you say. I wonder if you could find the exact wording in German? I'd like to know it, because he was recently deported from Canada on the basis of having been convicted under that law.

By the way, a propos of the possibility of the Allied atomic bombing of a German city, and of why the Americans bombed Hiroshima and Nagasaki: I don't think you are right. They did not do it for fun, or even to see if the bomb worked. They wanted to end the war quickly to save American lives. Their generals had estimated that it would cost one million American casualties to invade and subdue the Japanese main islands. This invasion would also have cost far more Japanese lives than the two atomic bombings. I think the dead of Hiroshima and Nagasaki were martyrs to the war crazies in the Japanese cabinet. Which does not absolve the Americans of their big share of blame for the policies that caused the war: that is the unresolved issue at the moment, I think.

J.

September 29, 1993

Dear Jim,

Yes, I'm quite prepared to ask myself (and tell you) what made me change tack after I had been a faithful follower of the Führer for half a dozen years or more.

From early boyhood I had flattered myself to be pretty intelligent and was convinced that by welcoming and admiring Hitler I had made a rational decision and not been swayed by circumstances and propaganda. A delusion, of course — but not quite. I read *Wilhelm Tell* when I was fifteen, and found that I was intrigued by the republicanism of the Swiss founding fathers. That troubled me somewhat. But I set my mind at rest by persuading myself that while a republic might be a great thing ideally, in practice, considering the notorious stupidity of the masses and the difficulty of ruling a big country, the Führer principle must prove superior. On a lower plane I let my critical faculties range freely to carp at what I thought were stupid faults of the government or the party. I enjoyed an imaginary risk of being mistaken for an enemy, knowing in my heart that if anything I was more Nazi than the common lot, bent on improving National Socialism. In short, when the end came, I was a young Nazi nut especially hard to crack.

The treatment we received at the hands of my American captors at Niederbreisig, Remagen, Sinzig, and Bolbec only confirmed my low opinion of what the victors stood for. It was only when at camp Philip Morris my English had sufficiently improved and I was in a position to pinch American books and newspapers clearly not tainted by re-educational hogwash that I got second thoughts about the fatherland and its enemies. I met an enlightened critical liberalism very much to my taste and completely lacking in the Germany I had loved. *The Republic* by Charles A. Beard became my staple, and Bill Mauldin's war cartoons, fair to the enemy and critical of Uncle Sam's own army, warmed my heart no end. Nothing remotely similar could have flowered under Hitler. I also read Thomas Mann's *Zauberberg (The Magic Mountain)*, and though only Volume II came my way then, the book has been a favourite with me ever since. It, too, opened vistas incompatible with what I knew made the Nazis tick.

And what about the death camps, the extermination of the Jews, you might ask. Didn't that contribute? Strange to say, that came much later. In the first ten years after the war, it was just a distant cloud hanging over me and the Germans in general. There was little reason or occasion for me and those I knew intimately to draw this horrible thing into our lives. You condemned it, everyone condemned it, but that was all. It didn't work a change in me, not the way Beard and Bill Mauldin had done. It took the rise of the neo-Nazis at the end of the 1950s for me to engage myself in the Christian-Jewish Society and dedicate an important part of my teaching life to battling neo-Nazism and antisemitism. After I'd been released from the PoW camps and my first contacts, in 1950, with an English university, its staff and students, and a whole year as "lecteur" at St. Andrews University, Scotland, the foundations of my political re-education were complete. In the early 1960s I found myself, somewhat to my surprise, well out in front against an all-too-immobile and reactionary Germany. Then, shortly after I had become a professor of English, Hannah Arendt with *On Revolution* influenced me more than any other political book after Charles A. Beard.

Of course you are right to spot a "generation" gap between us, simply because the years of our youth, our formative years, packed with history as they were, marched through our lives at a terrible pace. Thus a mere year's difference may in fact constitute something like a new generation. I notice this even when comparing notes with Germans about my age.

Again your letter gave me a lot to think about. How pertinent many of your remarks are. How open to counterattack my arguments sometimes seem to be. I notice you stick to your theory of German "fear," the theory that the Germans, most Germans or enough Germans, were so scared of the conquerors' wrath that they decided to suppress their memories of these conquerors' atrocities. That, you maintain, is the best explanation for German idealization of the Americans — psychologically perhaps along the line of kidnapper or hi-jack victims falling in love with these guys. Indeed it looks as if you had struck pure gold here: all "good behaviour" of post-war Germany can now neatly be reduced to a single cause: fear. Proof: now that the conquerors have left Germany, Nazism again raises its ugly head.

As beautiful an explanation as any reductionist explanation ever was! And how it cuts through all that nonsense about a new Germany, about German remorse and moral improvement!

I see what attracts you to it: first, its boldness, for you are bold by nature as well as profession (and I love you for it); second, it allows you to rally Germans to your cause by appealing to their pride; and third, and just by the by, you throw a reconciliatory bone to your old anti-Germanism, keeping in touch with the West's mainstream after all.

Meanwhile, you chose to overlook my own little explanation for why the Germans tend(ed) to spare the Americans. It was an inconspicuous explanation and lacked development, because at bottom I was, and still am, convinced that there is nothing to explain, really. What could be more in the course of nature, I thought, and still think, than that after so much futile straining and striving, after such material, emotional, and moral defeat and destruction a people should want to forget, to escape, to relax, to look after themselves, their immediate and medium-range needs? For six or more years they had sacrificed their individual plans, their normal lives, risked death a hundred times over, lost their health, their limbs, their sons, their brothers, their families, their houses, their homelands, their savings — well, almost anything you can think of — and all for some higher, collective purpose, for one's duty toward the greater good of one's country. What would standing up as witnesses of the camps, accusing America and France, have meant but going on sacrificing your health, your life, your peace in another collective cause, with little to gain, the unlikelihood of success under the circumstances staring you in the face?

That was the German "norm" and mainstream, I think, or what mainly contributed to it. Fear? That may have entered into it, okay. Even in individuals motives are mixed, let alone in a people of eighty million. I provided the example of the old pharmacist. But the relative unimportance of this is, I think, proved by the fact that the resolution to forget and refuse to answer questions about past horrors was even stronger in those who survived Russian camps. And these often haggard, ailing creatures, released into a Cold War Federal Republic certainly had nothing to fear from any occupation forces. There is also the fact that in those early years after the war this unwillingness to have anything to do with things beyond and above practical needs of the moment applied to the other side of the coin as well: only a tiny minority of Germans gratified the victors' and the Nazi victims' expectations of German feelings of guilt and remorse.

That, indeed, changed. With the passing of years, with the re-creation of normality, stability, and wealth in Germany, the voice of those calling for a collective sense of guilt, to be followed by appropriate words and deeds, gained strength and has in fact collectively won the day. And why, then, you will ask, did that new feeling of morality and justice not waken up the conscience of those who had buried their memories of the American and French (and Russian and Polish and Serb and Czech) post-war crimes against Germans? Well, because the process of suppressing and sealing these memories had acquired a new and much more principled justification. There are of course people, good and strong-minded people (and you among them, I think), who regard truth, morality, and justice as indivisible. What applies in one case, they insist, must apply in every other, regardless of who is to gain or lose.

I think from the early '60s onward the Germans discovered, as had rare individuals discovered before, that the happiness of individuals, as of nations, may call for the suspension of the indivisibility principle — suspension, that is, *by those who would profit from it.* Commonly the opposite happens: those to *lose* from the principle refuse to apply it; that's what is known as double standards, and against that the principle of indivisibility is an excellent antidote. But when Christ suggested that we desist from judging others, turn the other cheek, love our enemies, see the mote in our own eye and overlook the beam in the other's, he did ask us to divide morality. He invited us to subscribe to his other kind of "double standards," reversing the normal order of things. He taught: be strict with yourself, but loving and forgiving toward others.

That gained currency in German relations with the world, although only against bitter opposition from many Germans, from the German victims of Polish, Russian, Serb, and Czech ethnic cleansing. Girwert's letter to you and a letter of mine to the *FAZ* at the beginning of 1960 about how Germans should treat their guilt (which letter sent a wave of relief and applause even through that non-Left paper's readership) bear witness to that. It was the feeling that however unjust and unlawful the expulsion of the Germans from their old homelands and the accompanying atrocities had been, we should see all this in the light of what we had done to others and thereby break the chain of revenge and counter-reckoning and insist on the divisibility of justice for once. It should not surprise you that what applied to the East applied to the West all the more strongly. I'm not sure about Adenauer's case; I'm sure that it — and not cowardice — was behind Brandt's behaviour.

But the Nazis, you will remind me. How do I account for their reappearance despite all this German virtue?

When I was with you in June, several Canadians I met at a party asked me, What do you think of the new extreme Right in your country? What's happening to foreigners in Germany? Are you worried, Mr. Müller?

Well, Mr. Müller was. And more than that. And I said so. But why did I, and do I, find it so difficult to talk rationally and intelligibly about the subject?

It is because every time I open my mouth or put pen to paper, I have to react to two conflicting influences: the awful anti-foreigner attacks that happened in Rostock, Mölln, and Solingen — and may happen again in Germany — and the campaign against Germans and the German government because of them.

I'll try to forget this latter influence and concentrate on the surge of abominable violence against certain groups of foreigners in Germany and also against the homeless and the disabled.

Let me first state that this is the second time I have had to come to terms with this sort of thing. The original shock to my mental and emotional constitution came when in the late '60s a sizable part of the German public, mainly, though not exclusively, student, forced me to accept as a matter of fact as well as of principle that in order to get things done your way, you may fly in the face of civilized behaviour, deface any innocent surface of buildings, private or public, disturb the peace of any number of uninvolved people, insult, slander, and blackmail institutions and persons, using force whenever you think apt.

It was not so much these activities themselves that got me, not even when, in due time, they came to include arson and murder, but the offhandedness, the brazenness, the obvious pleasure that went with it, including the sympathies even for its terrorist version in some quarters, the snickering applause if the victims were hate figures for the Left. Having scruples, keeping within rules seemed all of a sudden nothing but old-fashioned.

This readiness to use violence survived when the '68 student revolution subsided. It turned into a politically neutralized, almost motive-free phenomenon, becoming more brutal and spreading to ever-younger age groups. A subculture of violence became a feature of German life, no-go areas documented the powerlessness of a police that the Left had ridiculed. By and by Germans learned that they probably had to accept this in a democracy determined not to turn into a police state.

That now the victims of that free-floating violence are increasingly coloured asylum seekers and Turks, that a branch of this subculture has taken a definitely racist and Nazi direction needs of course a more special explanation, but a general acceptance of violence is one element in what is happening in Germany today.

The prototypes of this skinhead movement in England were indeed triggered by racism, directed at Pakistani and West Indian immigrants, and the young Germans imitating the English used to be content, more or less, with provoking the contempt and anger of the rest of the German public by looking macho and Nazi with their old German uniforms and Nazi symbols, which in Germany were of course much more of a taboo breaker than anywhere else. That applied also and even more in the old GDR, where in the '80s young low-life escapism and protest looked with increasing envy and admiration at the possibilities in the West. But then this layer of German youth, revelling in self-gratification, in being different, in taboo breaking, booze, football stadium rowdyism and street fighting all of a sudden concentrated on the original skinhead enemy: foreigners. The liberated GDR gave the signal, and the rest of the German low-life young rallied to the cry.

Why did it start in the GDR and is still so much stronger in eastern Germany, where there are far fewer foreigners than in the west?

This is bound up with a feature of the liberated East that is little understood or deliberately ignored in the West. It was, I think, no accident that even normal decent people stood by, watching and even spurring on the hooligans attacking the asylum seekers' houses in Rostock. It's the phenomenon of strict coercive education, suddenly relaxed. They had bowed to communist police state moralizing and bullying for decades. And now like schoolboys released from the regimen of hard taskmasters, they run riot first thing. In a way they simply took the Western promise of a land of freedom seriously. For weeks those Gypsies from Romania had taken over their peaceful neighbourhood, had feasted all night, defecated into the Germans' front gardens, and the authorities, if appealed to, had shrugged their shoulders. That was not these East Germans' idea of life in a new Germany. If someone offered to help them get rid of such "guests" they couldn't remember inviting, they wouldn't be choosy.

The same thing happened, at a higher level, when several weeks later a committee, including Herr Ignatz Bubis, the chairman of the Central Council of Jews in Germany, arrived in Rostock to assess the situation, and one of the city councillors was so infuriated by what he saw as the highfalutin condescension of these people that he asked Herr Bubis sharply if it was correct that he was a citizen of Israel, and would it not be a good idea for him to look into that country's behaviour among Palestinians instead of ticking off a German city council that had enough problems as it was. Unthinkable that anything like that could have happened at Solingen or Mölln or anywhere else in western Germany. Even under a much more extreme provocation, an official here would think twice before risking a word that might be construed as antisemitic. East Germans are different. In a way they are endearingly naive. For decades they used to suppress their spontaneity, hedge their language, calling the Russian masters "friends" and observing all the taboos surrounding official communist doctrine and practice. They simply can't see why now, in an allegedly free country, they should still be afraid to raise their heads and speak their minds.

And exactly that has of course been the burden of the German Right in the west since 1945. This Right does not feed on dreams of returning to Hitler. That's only the stick the Left and the Centre like to beat them with. What really has kept them going is a sense of victimization, of suppression of feelings and ideas that they think ought to be legitimate in a free country. It's the refusal to be forced to think and speak ill of your fathers and forefathers, or to see Nazism as simply black and everything else, including communism, as white. They are furious at the German media and the rest of the world telling the Germans with one voice how little they are up to scratch morally, or at politicians bootlicking in Poland and Israel and giving hundreds of billions of Deutschmarks and even German land to these countries, or falling over their feet to merge the fatherland in a faceless Europe. In short, the German Right stands very much for normal unrefined thinking of run-of-the-mill people all over the world — except that such normality was never a viable option in an abnormal post-war Germany. The more thinking, realistic, and far-seeing political leaders of the main parties knew that; they understood the German position in the world after the Nazi abominations. And till very recently the Germans have voted for them, not for the extreme Right, and increasingly so, because partly they too had come to see the light of higher morality, partly because on balance swallowing one's national pride seemed miraculously to pay off nationally, giving the lie to the inveterate tempters from the Right.

That this is changing, that right-wing parties, at least the more civilized brands like the "Republicans," are making headway at elections after all, can thus be put down to the fact that increasingly the rewards of being "good," that is, altruistic, European, cosmopolitan, after reaching a late and already flawed peak in reunification are now less and less in evidence for more and more people.

This is exacerbated by the fact that politics, no matter who is at the helm, has become so difficult that people are becoming frustrated and furious about the established political class, which they think is not willing or able to solve the ever-more-pressing problems. They don't see that one of the reasons for the immobility that has seized German politics in the face of ever-greater challenges lies in themselves. Never before have they divided so evenly on so many issues, and without being aware of this, because the dividing line no longer squares with party lines. Everybody is sure to know what ought to be done, and everybody knows lots of people who think like him or her, so that he or she cannot imagine that another equally large number of Germans should think the very opposite. Thus every proposal gets caught up somewhere on its way through the constitutional institutions. There are no longer any clear majorities to steer things successfully through the intricate system of German checks and balances, with Brussels and all kinds of powerful unparliamentary veto groups, like farmers and trades unions, thrown in for good measure. Take abortion, take health and old-age-care financing, take crime, drugs and the mafia, take recession, take unemployment, take the role of the German army outside NATO, take ... foreigners.

Well, there we are again: foreigners. That's the issue on which all explanatory strands I have mentioned unite most fatefully.

But, dear Jim, I feel exhausted. I think I'll call it a day, although there is so much left to say.

Just one more point in your last letter I'd like to put straight. I didn't mean to say that all or most German soldiers were Nazi. My English must have failed me there. What I intended to transmit was that I can imagine there having been three different groups of German PoWs, the last being Nazi, but all having their different respective reasons for lacking feelings of guilt.

R.

November 22, 1993

Dear Richard,

My goodness, you are the bold one. Reductionist, indeed.

It is not the boldness of the explanation that appeals to me. In fact, I am appalled to think of the Germans as so beaten that they will not

*defend themselves. Can this be good for the minorities under the influence
of Germans? Can the weak trust someone to defend them who will not
defend himself? This is why I insist on the importance of Germans denouncing the atrocities of the Allies. You Germans are thinking of guilt,
not goodness. You are lost in the contemplation of your own fantastic
evil. I fancy I can even hear it in the deeply gloomy tones of the German-
speaking voice: when I call Europe on the phone, I know the English-
speaking German operators not mainly by their accent but more by the
slow sad tone. A tone, by the way, that is missing from your voice, and
Hilla's. That was one of the ways that I knew I could get along with you,
and discuss this subject honestly. Your voice has very little of that melancholy in it. I thought you were absolutely free of pointless guilt, that you
had met it, and suffered, and were now the better for it.*

When I began the research for my latest book, Just Raoul, *it was
because I had heard so much about the guilty acts of the Germans, killing
off so many civilians. I was sick of atrocity. I thought, What good comes
from studying evil? And then I read* Avenue of the Righteous, *by Peter
Hellmann, of New York. He described the righteous Christians who had
saved many Jews from the Nazis during the war. Among them was Raoul
Laporterie of Grenade-sur-l'Adour near Bordeaux, who had saved many
hundreds of the persecuted from the Nazis during the war. My book about
this charming, brave, beautiful man was published to a few good reviews
in the U.S.A. and Canada, but in Germany no one would touch it. My
previous book with Ullstein was a best-seller, and publishers love to follow
up an author's best-seller with another book, but not this one. If it were
true that the Germans had really repented, they would want to read about
someone who had with courage and humour, defied the bestial Nazis,
someone who had mocked their ferocity, saved hundreds of people, and
lived to tell his story. If they hated evil now, and loved the good, or at
least knew what was good and wanted some of it for themselves, they
would have wanted this book. But no, they are apparently interested in
crime, not decency. Ullstein was absolutely convinced that it was pointless
to try to sell that book in Germany. My agent didn't even want to try to
sell it. The Germans wanted only* Other Losses/Der Geplante Tod,
*with its record of crime and horror against them. Today, the Germans
have paid their reparations, they weep when they get off the gleaming tour
busses in Wroclaw (Breslau) and see the mess the drunken Poles have
made of prosperous Silesia. And they apologize over and over to whoever
wants to come to Germany to abuse them for the millionth time, American, Israeli, British, French — anyone can come. But only because you*

are still playing the loser. One of the best German films of recent times was Das schreckliche Mädchen (The Nasty Girl), about a German girl in the 1980s who inadvertently digs up the truth about her town's Nazi past. It had been hidden by these good Germans you want me to believe are filled with regret and have improved themselves. You have, Richard, and many have, but many have not, I am sure. Otherwise, how could such a film have been made and become popular? Why would Der Geplante Tod *sell, but not* Just Raoul?

And there is the veterans' magazine put out by the Verband der Heimkehrer,* *which circulates to over 250,000 subscribers every issue, still, in the 1990s, but it has hardly ever published an article about the death camps of Eisenhower and de Gaulle. It is all about the vile Soviets. Yet there were four times as many prisoners in the West as in the East, and their conditions in the West were even worse, for a long time. So for years this magazine has been printing anti-Soviet truth and propaganda, while completely ignoring the Western atrocities. In fact, most Germans blame the Western atrocities on the Soviets by saying that yes, so many died, but they died in the East. This goes on all the time — one of the chief protagonists of this is Prof. Art Smith of California, who says that a survey conducted by the Germans found that the great majority of war prisoners who were missing were last seen on the Eastern Front, concluding from this that most of the missing 1.7 million died in Soviet camps. Well, I talked to Dr. Margarethe Bitter of Munich, who was in charge of that survey, and she told me that this was not true, that they had no idea where the prisoners were after the war. Yet a German publisher of repute published Smith's allegations again, in 1993, though they are completely false. A phone call to Dr. Bitter would have established the truth for Smith's editor, but it was not made. Who can explain this? This is a deliberate blindness.*

It may have had a spurious justification during the Cold War, because our minds were drugged with propaganda to keep us hating the enemy, but that has not been necessary now for years. The time is here to tell the truth, before we all die out of time.

Surely this is not the forgetting that you are talking about; this is a political act of false remembering. It proceeds more from pure prejudiced hatred of all Bolshevism than from a need to reveal the truth about their atrocities. It is fundamentally very like Nazi propaganda all over again. How could such things happen, if Germany were as you believe?

---

* *Association of returned veterans.*

The way out of evil is to learn goodness, not to rehearse guilt.

My impression is that today Germans twist their necks to avoid seeing any "moral aspect" of events inside or outside the country. (I put that in quotes because it is such a vague term, meaning, for me, good and evil, the things you don't want done to yourself that you sometimes want to do to others.) Since morality in the West often means proclaiming the right to condemn others, we can see how far it goes by finding out who in Germany condemns others. But no, you are almost entirely free of that. There is nothing today in the German national policy or character to compare with the British hypocrisy under the title the White Man's Burden, or the French under the Mission Civilisatrice, *or the hypocritical outrage of President Bush and others confronted with Saddam Hussein, condemning him as another Hitler, or Reagan calling the U.S.S.R. "the Evil Empire." This sort of thing goes on all the time over here, whereas it seems to me you are now comparatively free of it. Our leaders are always telling us about the Evil One in the world whose nasty plans we must smash before he smashes us. Or if the Evil One is no direct threat to us, then he is another Hitler, or he is breaking some ideal of the world that we have, which must be defended. Then of course anyone who reveals that we ourselves are always breaking that ideal is silenced, or beaten up, or whatever.*

Since you Germans got rich again, we in the rest of the West have sent out soldiers and money to save democracy or freedom or whatever time and again, while you stayed home enjoying your philistine wealth. This was not just because your constitution forbids foreign adventures; you could have given far more money than you did. Enlighten me if I am ignorant here, please, but I have the strong impression that the spirit of the German people today is depressed. In post-war German art, literature, film, music, philosophy, very little enlightens or refreshes you, or the rest of the world. It's all so melancholy. Your great Bertolt Brecht took his inspiration not from the reincarnation of the German spirit in guilty humility after 1945, but from the ancient hatred Marx felt for German capitalism and the hope he felt in socialism. Heinrich Böll, I think, may be the sole exception to what I just said, and he was refreshing because he was so funny.

Of course you are right that Germans wanted to put it all behind them, but I think it was because you lost the war. The guilt came after. This does not mean that in general when you were winning the war you countenanced widely known Nazi atrocities, but rather that these atrocities were successfully covered up from most Germans for the greater part of the war. I think that to hide such things is inevitable, because one fears retribution. But I do not think that you would say that to hide these things was good, would you? And if it is not, surely the Germans today have the duty to bear witness against the crimes of the conquerors, which have so far been mainly covered up in the West. Not one person in ten thousand over here knows anything about the vast crimes committed against you by the Western allies under the Morgenthau Plan, although we suspected that grisly things were being done to you by the Evil Empire. It is precisely because most of the Germans have accepted these crimes as inevitable, and therefore close to normal, that they are not known here. And there is another gruesome parallel with the Nazis. Crimes that are regarded as inevitable come to seem normal. Surely the Nazis found it easier to mask their crimes because most of the people who did know about them thought that the crimes were somehow "normal." The German government has for decades now been publishing statistics showing that in the year 1947, when as everyone knows there was famine imposed on your country by the conquerors, and people literally falling over dead in the streets from starvation, and people lived six to a small basement room without enough coal, thinly dressed in winter, in that year, the death rate was 12.1 per thousand, which was less than the death rate (12.2) the same government reports for the years 1968-69 of the Wirtschaftswunder (the German post-war economic miracle). Yes indeed, those are the numbers your government publishes and gives to schoolchildren. You've got to hand it to those Germans, don't you? Imagine being able to live longer while starving to death. I don't know how they do it, unless by the magic of statistics.

You don't have to do a moment's research to realize that the 1947 figure is wrong, but there it is, officially published for forty years. And where did those statistics for 1947 come from? Why, the conquerors, of course. But you don't have to repeat their propaganda, do you? Thus your suffering is denied repeatedly by official cover-up.

Yet you have a law to prevent anyone from defaming the memory of the dead, to preserve the memory of the persecution of the Jews. And here your own government breaks that law and has been breaking it for forty years.

I have just returned from the Hoover Institution at Stanford, where I was doing research for my (other) new book. Before going, I had read Konrad Adenauer's memoirs (Erinnerungen), in which he wrote, "According to American figures, a total of 13.3 million Germans were expelled from the eastern parts of Germany, from Poland, Czechoslovakia, Hungary, and so on. 7.3 million arrived in the Eastern (Soviet) zone and the three western zones, most of these in the latter. Six million Germans have disappeared from the earth. They are dead, gone.[16] *I did not believe this until I began to study the figures at Stanford, among files that were classified until 1988, and that as far as I can tell have never been published in any form. Studying these files, which were assembled by Dr. Behnke of the U.S. Army in Germany, and by Ambassador Robert Murphy, I was slowly convinced that Dr. Adenauer was right. In fact, he probably understated the number of deaths, all due to the expulsions, the rape, murder, beating, and starvation of the expellees starting as the war ended. When one compares the results of the censuses of 1946 and 1950, one sees that five million people more than normal died in Germany in those years, and that their deaths went unrecorded by the Allies, who were in charge of the statistics.*

I flew back across the continent looking down on the farms and cities of all the people, many still alive, who had done some of these things. It was all very peaceful and beautiful — hard to imagine that there were war criminals walking around down there who had wilfully contributed to the deaths of millions of your people in peacetime. And on the same farms that I could see squared off, all with the pale, pinky haze of ripe autumn on them, was grown the wheat that saved millions of Germans, because of the decency of the far greater number of the Canadians and Americans who worked hard and gave up much so that your people could outlive the dull cruelty of the Morgenthau Plan. What tremendous earthly power was down there, what conflict between the good and evil that men do.

What has shocked me almost as much as the list of incredible crimes has been the reaction among Germans when I tell them of what I am finding. The head of the German Canadian Congress said, when I told him how many had died, "I'm not surprised." A very successful German-Canadian businessman who escaped from Königsberg to Canada in 1948, thanks to a friendly Canadian major, said, "Yes, that's right." And you told me on the phone just now that you thought the figure was true (or some such).

Richard, these are astounding crimes, widely known but hardly ever discussed in Germany, and then only in tones of sad regret mixed with guilt — there's that tone again — and never in outrage. You and we pay them no attention, while we scrutinize every skinhead rally or crime in

16 Konrad Adenauer, Memoirs, 1945-1953, Chicago, Regnery, 1966. Deutsche Verlags-Anstalt, p. 48.

Germany today. After I got back here, Elisabeth had ready for me a story in the paper about skinheads beating up foreigners in Germany. I am sure that the crimes of the Allies after the war are at the heart of much German xenophobia today. The skinhead who beats up a foreigner has been told what happened to his grandmother in the Stuttgart subway tunnels in 1945 when the French army let its black colonial troops loose there. Perhaps the xenophobic reaction is most violent in eastern Germany because the worst crimes were committed against Germans in areas bordering that part of Germany, and by Soviets.

As I see it, you are sunk in a comfortable guilt. It is easy to bear now, because it has become part of your system of life — to pay the reparations, make the apologies, grovel before the critics, stay out of international affrays, avoid the truth in art and history. You are like the prisoner devoted to his chains. Your state of mind, I suggest, is not good, it is easy. Easier to stay as you are than to deal with one of the main roots of today's neo-Nazi recrudescence. But you are never going to solve that problem — in fact, it will only get worse — if the poison goes on contaminating your German bloodstream. There, I've said it, German blood. Und der Boden *is getting into* das Blut.

Something almost incredible happened during the opening ceremonies of the Holocaust Museum in Washington earlier this year. The director refused to honour the Germans who during the war had tried to save the lives of German Jews from Hitler's persecution. The museum had announced several years ago a symposium of academics to occur in honour of the opening. Hearing of this, a very distinguished German scholar wrote to the museum to say that he would be glad to help organize a display about the German resistance to Hitler's regime during the war. This resistance was partly defined by hatred of what Hitler was doing to the Jews and others. These highly-placed officers risked and lost their lives in a resistance that for them had been caused mainly or entirely by the suffering of their fellow citizens. There was no mention of the subject of resistance at the opening ceremonies. Thus, those who did honour to their nation have been ignored once again, by the people who owed most to them. The revisionists against the Holocaust seem to have been joined by a new clan, the revisionists against the Germans.

The point about this, of course, is that it shows how the contempt of the West for the Germans has been carried into the 1990s, and only a few Germans have ever protested. The German embassy in Washington said nothing, the people at Yad Vashem said nothing in public, and no

German group in North America has ever commented on the failure to deplore the Museum's indifference to these brave people. But anyone thinking of blaming the Jews has to ask first, Why are the Germans themselves indifferent? You wallow in guilt and ignore the good you did. And this is exactly what the French do to this day. They are wrongfully accused of doing nothing to save their fellow Jews during the war, when the fact is that the French saved over 90 per cent of their native-born Jews. The semi-fascist Vichy regime collapsed in front of German antisemitism and allowed the Germans to send off to Auschwitz the majority of refugee Jews in the country. The French to this day pay the price in guilt and shame for Vichy, but almost no one has honoured those incredibly brave French people — hundreds of thousands of them, perhaps millions — who risked their lives, their houses, their food, to shelter French Jews in their homes for years. It is a story almost totally ignored in France, in favour of French self-abasement. Again, if honour is not respected, dishonour will take its place, at least among the racists in France and Germany. And this is a great deal of the source of the hatred of the refugees and immigrants in both countries. Perfect guilt casteth out love.

Are you Germans so sunk in sloth and guilt and love of money that you do not even know you are being dishonoured? If you don't care about the people who showed you the light, you don't care about the light. The darkness comes again.

On the fifty-fifth anniversary of Kristallnacht, which I helped to celebrate a little by attending the speech of a survivor at Lodzer Holocaust Centre in Toronto, there was also a different kind of ceremony. This one was in front of the German consulate in Toronto, close to my grandfather's house. People who would not identify themselves demonstrated in front of the big old house carrying signs denouncing German racism, the Germans as murderers. The following night, the Toronto police failed to protect the consulate from attacks by vandals who flung paint all over the door and surrounding wall.

All those who are now in power in Germany, and all their predecessors for forty-five years, have denounced the crimes of the Nazis. They are vigorous in pursuit of neo-Nazis, revisionists, rightists in general, far more than are, say, the Americans, who still allow revisionists the right to express themselves freely in print, on radio, and TV. These same German government officials are in charge of the greatest reparations program the world has ever known, over 100 billion D-marks to date, and counting. Nearly all of this has gone to Jewish victims of Nazi persecution. This program, far from winding down as victims die, recently expanded by decision of the German government to include victims of the Nazis in East Germany who had never before been compensated.

This is the government whose officers are reviled and decried, whose buildings are attacked and vandalized. And what do they do in protest? Nothing. The Toronto police, having failed to prevent the attack, failed to find, or even to attempt to find, the criminals. No Toronto paper reported the attack or the demonstration. Nothing was reported on radio or TV. And the German Canadian Congress, having discussed the event, decided to do nothing. For them, it was just one small event in a long, sad story.

Now, the world howls at the Germans for doing so little to defend the Turkish victims in Solingen and elsewhere. If the Germans won't defend their own doorway in Toronto, why would they defend Turks?

I returned from research at the Hoover Institution one night in October and had this dream the next afternoon: I was in a sort of castle where lots of beer was stored in huge brown wooden barrels. I suspected that something important was hidden in one of them, and I managed to persuade the castle authorities against their will to let me take one barrel out. The horses pulled a cart loaded with the barrel over the cobblestones of the courtyard, but it rolled off, cracked open, the beer flowed out, and there on the wood rested a perfect set of golden human teeth. I have a feeling those teeth are what I found in Stanford, and they are going to bite the ankles of a lot of liars and mythmakers who have been making a nice business out of German bashing. Well, there it is for now. Your friend with the golden teeth,

J.

December 17, 1993

Dear Jim,

I hear the trumpets of the Angel of the Last Judgment in your letter of November 22. I also sense the exasperation of the proto-American: the brave, the optimistic, the common-sensically good guy, rooted in a vast new country, nature still glorious at his side, seeing us over here, especially us Germans, weak, meek, narrow-minded, melancholy, enslaved, unstraightforward, caught in a net of collective falsehoods.

In a curious twist of historic perspective, it reminded me of reck-less Lord Byron depicting the patience and apathy with which the Greeks were bearing the Turkish yoke, unmindful of their glorious past. How he tried to shame them into action, make them see the unworthiness of their petty existence!

There seems, then, not only to be a generation gap between us but also a clash of cultures. We are evidently in need of a two-way translation of basic unspoken concepts. Yes, Germany lost the war, we were beaten. In fact we lost two big wars in a lifetime against the same enemies. That's the truth. And you say that's what's at the bottom of our collective state of mind still. Thinking it over for a while, I agree. At the very bottom, what else could there be?

But I won't allow Lord Bacque (Lord Jim?) to denounce the collective state of the German mind wholesale because of this par-entage. Defeat may indeed slap you down for good; it may, inciden-tally, also spur you on to new attempts at victory, as was the case with post-First World War Germany; but it may also teach you to shift your points of reference and turn you into something else, some-thing new and — hopefully — better. At the end of the day, even guilt may be a blessing — a "felix culpa." Now that's talking loftily and in the abstract. You prefer a hard, practical look at today's Germans, and practicing that look you don't find anything new or better. In fact, you find us wanting on almost all counts.

Now I won't say you are just wrong or that you don't know your Germans. (You certainly seem to have a good ear for the tone of national voices.) I myself have accumulated quite a bit of ire against my countrymen (and myself) in the course of a lifetime, and some of it quite along your line: that particular kind of undignified grov-elling, self-deprecation, and slavish falling over your feet to ingrati-ate yourself with victors and victorious tendencies of one sort or another.

I just received a written report by a former inmate of Remagen PoW camp who deemed it appropriate to insert a forelock-tugging remark about how highly he thought of the Americans for not rid-ding him of his wedding ring (only of all other valuables)!

But isn't virtue always shadowed by its caricature? And hypocrisy, doesn't it at least nod at standards-in-being it dare not openly defy? I at least know enough Germans — and their number has grown over the years — simple and not-so-simple folk including politicians, whose well-meaning moral nature in politics and collective ethics command my respect. Quite a few of them are women. They may not be all to my taste, they may be "too German" in some way, too much caught up in a guilt syndrome, and I may even think them politically wrong-headed, but they are a good stabilizing element in the makeup of post-war Germany, especially valuable just now when the xenophobic Right imagined it was on the verge of power, and then to its surprise found tens of thousands of these decent Germans mourning with the Turks in silent candlelight processions. I should hate these earnest people to be made fun of or discouraged, just as I would hate to see the extreme Right encouraged by your philippic. You think we have been choosing the easy way, not the good way. I understand what you mean, I appreciate your ideal. It is highly moral *and* anti-philistine, peacefully humanitarian *and* militant. But it's an ideal, and not everything falling short of an ideal is therefore to be despised. There are worse things than people choosing the easy way, and there is a streak of the puritan in you who thinks that what is easy cannot be good.

As I have said before, I have come to hesitate before belittling something in the name of an ideal, or to use ideals to bring down what modest good has fortunately grown up. Most people are not born to be heroes, and many first need encouragement and to be told how to go about it. I agree we should praise the model people and the model deeds. Let nobody denounce the Laporteries as do-gooders or whatever. But let us at the same time acknowledge normal life of normal people, even if they are Germans, who, like most people around the world, are most of the time neither particularly good nor particularly bad. Let's try to tease them into becoming better but not give it to them with a sledgehammer. And then, even some ideals may be out of place sometimes, or ought to be preached with caution. In general and as an individual I would subscribe to your ideal — I mean, standing up to any injustice whatever, defending truth quietly but courageously, whether the victim is yourself or somebody else. But when one speaks of a nation, speaks of Germany or "the Germans," speaks *to* them as a writer, or as a politician, a high ideal may in the event turn rather sour, may in their ears and hands become something very far from what you or I had in mind. A nation, a national mind, is a big and complex thing, and it's not easy to change its course, let alone change it precisely as you would wish it to change. Calling on its sensibilities, on "manly" virtues of defending its "rights," its "honour," calling on its fighting spirit, may be all too successful in the end. Isn't there a cautionary English saying, Let well enough alone?

As for German leading statesmen: there have been quite a number since the war who were a far cry from the cowardly guilt-ridden type whom you consider dominant in Germany. Konrad Adenauer, Kurt Schumacher, Ludwig Erhard, Gustav Heinemann, Franz Josef Strauss and Helmut Schmidt immediately spring to mind. In their encounters with the victors and the victims, they never forgot the manly ideal you evoke and acted accordingly. But toward their electorate, these same politicians knew better than to whip up feelings of national pride and resentment, however much such feelings were justified by anti-German deeds and words of the post-war world. And wouldn't even you loathe to feel in any way responsible for the German tanker veering from too much meekness toward aggressiveness, an aggressiveness almost by necessity escalating in the face of an equally foreseeable world resistance to it? Of course your onslaught is now driving me into a corner I don't feel is truly mine — not in Germany at any rate, not toward Germans. While indeed insisting on the merits of German guilt consciousness and atonement, I, too, feel that this has not always taken the best form possible, and that with time its side effects may be accumulating to something positively dangerous. That's where we meet, though with different accentuations and conclusions. I too see a connection between the post-war tradition of German submissiveness and the recent rise of the Far Right. While the Left and the Jews think that this just shows a sad slackening of the spirit of penance, etc., on the part of the Germans, I know that the shoe is on the other foot. If there has been any weakening of the spirit of guilt acknowledgement it's because of its overapplication, its nauseating repetitious hectoring and sloganeering, its unbearable pathos that has made too many Germans — and most of the young — either "mother deaf," i.e., immune to anything sounding that tiresome bell, or positively mad at it. You believe the skins *et al.* attack foreigners because they have been listening to what their grandparents told them about what foreigners did to German men and women in 1945 and subsequently. I think that a bit far-fetched or short circuited, but taken in the wider sense of hurt patriotism, of being ashamed of an apparent lack of guts in German politics, it's probably correct. (It isn't much use asking them. They'll tell you anything you want if you pay them handsomely. And they enjoy the way the media and the world see them as the true — i.e., shocking — Germans.)

What really gives the neo-Nazis political clout today is the foreigner question, the question of that faction seeing Germany overrun and overwhelmed by all manner of low-life or black foreigners, in the way the racist politician Enoch Powell in his famous "rivers of blood" speech ten years ago envisaged things would turn out in Great Britain.

On the question of counter-strategies against the neo-Nazis, political opinion in Germany is sharply and sadly divided. One half maintains and convinces itself that the inrush of foreigners is no problem and that anyone talking of it as a problem is creating the problem and thus plays into the hands of the neo-Nazis. The other half thinks that certain groups of foreigners are indeed a problem, or that at least enough of the German electorate considers them a problem, and that just by denying it you drive these into the fold of the neo-Nazis. By denying the existence of a problem, the former group — roughly half the social democrats, half the CDU and half the FDP (Freie Demokratische Partei-Liberals) — incapacitates itself politically, because its room for action is restricted to shooing away evil fantasies of the Right. In order to compensate for that weakness, they would probably like to complement the law against the Auschwitz-lie by a law punishing the foreigner-invasion lie. They think, or at least profess to think, that it is neither just nor possible for the people called Germans, living in a country called Germany, to prevent any non-German human from setting up camp among them, no matter what kind he or she is or what numbers in what period of time are involved. This is in fact, though not by intent, part of the German constitution, which works out as a general invitation to any needy foreigners to come and enjoy the benefits of settling in Germany.

Now if you take a very long or wide view, there is indeed no valid argument against any kind of immigration. Even if mass immigration should damage the lives of the people forming the host nation, and even if it should at last cause many of them to leave the country they no longer recognize as theirs and immigrate in turn to places more congenial to their ways and customs, after a couple of centuries it's all history with new facts and new problems commanding everybody's attention. But in the short or middle term I consider it's legitimate for a given population to decide about foreigners' entry into their country.

It is, of course, to be wished that all countries have an open heart for those in need of ayslum. But I don't think that asylum, i.e., asylum in a foreign country, can be a *right*. A constitutional law giving every outsider a statutory right to settle in Germany regardless of unforeseeable numbers, costs, circumstances is legal nonsense.

And why do the Germans have such a law or, rather, laws that have come to amount to just that? You may well ask. Until very recently I shared your assumption that it owed its existence to German moral hubris: repenting of their evil past, they tried to go it one better than the rest of the world. But I have always had difficulty in explaining (to myself and others) why this proud achievement appeared in the strange context of paragraph 16 of our constitution. And now a new and perhaps more credible explanation has come up. According to one Johannes Munier, Berlin (in a letter to the *FAZ* of June 5, 1993), its origins were less lofty than we both assumed. It seems to have been put in as an afterthought and in order to be better able to defend ourselves against the dictatorships of the world, especially the Eastern Communists, who might consider the German practice of freely admitting fugitives from their countries as "unfriendly acts," charging the Germans (and the whole West; but only the Germans were in their grip) with aggressively seducing their nationals into deserting the Workers' Paradise. If part of the constitution, this would be beyond actual politics. We could then say, Sorry, it's nothing to do with you in particular; it's in our *Grundgesetz.* So, for all its hyper-moral potential, the foundation of the tagged-on sentence seems to have been Cold War.

After we'd seen years of wrangling and giving the neo-Nazis a surefire case, a reform of this asylum law was at last effected this year, needing as it did a two-thirds majority in Parliament, and I, and most German politicians when the mikes are off, hope that this reformed paragraph will in practice amount to something like the removal of the thing. But a vociferous, radical, media-occupying movement has attacked the change as Nazi, as final proof, if proof was needed, that the real perpetrators of the crimes against foreigners sit in Bonn.

But to return to your letter.

Pardon me for saying so, but you seem to me blind to your very achievements. You are the one who has discovered and researched a horrible story. You have presented it to an unbelieving world, including an unbelieving Germany. You are slowly forcing the world and Germany to accept that there may be something in what you say. But instead of being justly proud of this and by and by reaping its fruits, you are in danger of marring it all by now maintaining that in fact there had been nothing to discover, that all along the truth had been there for everybody to see, that in fact everybody had seen it, but for all kinds of unseemly reasons had turned their eyes away.

But that's not the truth, not to the extent you think it's the truth, and even if it were, what good do you expect from ramming it down people's throats at this point in time?

You write that *Der Heimkehrer* published articles about the death camps of the Soviets and not about the death camps of Eisenhower. (And of course this was the case also with other German newspapers and magazines.) But however much that may have been influenced by anti-communist prejudice, old or new, it was also what this magazine and everybody else believed. Why should they have doubted this "knowledge" before you came along to prove it wrong?

And to be fair, I still believe that there were unspeakable horrors German prisoners went through in Russia. For most prisoners in American custody, the nightmares of Kreuznach, Sinzig, Rheinhausen, etc. ended at some time in 1945. If these horror camps did not kill them, they were released, turned over to the French (which is another story), or sent to one of the American labour camps, which, though illegal, were anything but death camps. By contrast, the misery of the German prisoners in Russia went on for years and years. Look at the pictures of those released in the 1950s!

I am very much interested in what you found out while probing into the archives of the Hoover Institution, but I tremble somewhat at the rashness with which you appear to embrace the number of six million dead in the course of the expulsion in 1945. Aren't you the slightest bit afraid of becoming James "Big Numbers" Bacque?

What seems to me an honest account, prejudiced, if at all, in your direction, was published in 1982 by Heinz Nawratil (*Vertreibungsverbrechen an Deutschen*, Ethnic cleansing crimes against Germans), who, after consulting the published sources, comes to the conclusion that no exact death figures can be given, but that we can safely say that the number was about 3 million. (The number usually given is 2.8 million.) The book's strength, it is true, lies in its unairbrushed factual reports, its pictures, and its open language, not in statistical research. So I don't doubt that there is room for new discoveries. But unless you are very sure of your material (Adenauer's assumptions count little in themselves), I wouldn't climb out on a limb with this. And don't overrate that Germans "think such a figure possible." It only proves a point you make against them: that apart from the *Vertriebenenverbände*,* they chose not to face the facts.

The Germans who were expelled from east of the Oder and from Bohemia indeed paid the cost of German atonement in terms of non-remembrance. After their horrible experience, they were asked to remain silent and watch their experience being wiped from the national slate. But the decisive motives for this were rational and moral, even if mistaken: an open, collective visualizing of the crimes committed by Russians, Poles, Czechs, Yugoslavs, accompanied as it would have been by howling anti-German campaigns from these countries flatly denying the charges, and the Western press wagging their heads over the fascist aggressors getting cheeky again, seemed unlikely to allow us to come to terms, morally and politically, with a post-war world of victims and victors and the narrow place we might at best hope to occupy in it.

I too find it hard to stomach the outrageous story of the Holocaust Museum refusing acknowledgement of anything that might lift the black shadow it cannot help throwing on Germans from here to eternity. You may or may not know that our government pleaded for months with those running this German-horror show to include at least a token appreciation of what the new Germany has done to make amends, which the world at large knows almost nothing of. They wouldn't even consider it. But they then frowned at the German president, Richard von Weizsäcker, who refused to follow their invitation to the opening ceremony!

Well, let's hear of the good people of the world and the good deeds that humanity is capable of, after all. What a pity that the Germans are barred from reading about just Raoul Laporterie. But after eighteen publishing houses explaining to me why for one reason or another or none at all they would rather not run the risk of publishing *my* book, I won't even pretend to understand what keeps Ullstein from publishing that story. I loved it.

R.

---

* Association of Expellees

April 2, 1994

Dear Richard,

You write so well, you think so clearly, you have such a broad range of knowledge that sometimes I think I should write only just enough to provoke a reply from you, then sit back to enjoy it. But I have to work overtime instead to keep up with your energetic and illuminating responses.

All right, enough of the prisoner's last meal; now to hang you.

I was stunned to read the history of the supposedly generous German law on immigration. What a contrast between the grim reality of the reason and the warm praise that resulted. How odd life is, that forgotten events change our lives. As Eliot said, "Rust that clings to the form that the strength has left,/Hard and curled and ready to snap."

And we lose truth because of it.

You did not answer my point re the impossibility of Germans' defending minorities if they will not defend themselves. So I will suggest a line of reasoning to you. There is no necessary connection. A people may defend itself ardently but at the same time, perceiving an enemy within its borders, persecute a minority. This was what Hitler did.

Another example of this in history is the North Americans and the aborigines. We North Americans defend ourselves very well, even where we have not really been attacked, i.e., when we wage a war of ideals, as, for instance, against the communists, but at the same time we have persecuted the aborigines mercilessly. Especially bad were those great idealists, the Americans. There is no defence of minorities that is essential to the collective self-interest of the majority, and possibly even the reverse is true. Still it does remain an interesting point, if not about how to defend ideals, at least how to understand German idealism today, since one of Germany's ideals is the need to atone to the victims. In a nutshell, that is all I am saying about us in the English-speaking democracies too, you know: we should admit our guilt and atone to our victims too.

The Germans are savagely criticized in Western capitals for the attacks on immigrants, but we in the West now pretend to admire the heroic resistance to immigration put up by other peoples in other times. The best argument against mass immigration into Germany today is clearly made by the aborigines of the Americas. Because of our immigration, their ancestors suffered the greatest genocide in human history, which has been going on for five centuries, and flared up again just last week with the

Chiapas rebellion in Mexico. People all over the West sympathize with the Yanomami of the Amazon basin in their struggle to prevent immigration. There was even a flare-up in Canada two summers ago, when the Canadian army confronted the Mohawks of the Kahnesetake reserve near Montreal, trying to defend a land grab by the local white people. And of course the suicides and premature deaths of natives on reserves all over North America bespeak the poverty and distress of their present way of life, much of it induced by contact with the white peoples who have not usually kept the promises made to the aboriginals when the land was first acquired.

All of this is a leftover of the failed resistance to immigration put up by hundreds of thousands of aborigines who saw clearly that their way of life would be destroyed if they did not resist.

And now we in the West make heroes of the Iroquois, Aztecs, Maya, Inca, Sioux, and so on who tried to save their nations by preventing us from immigrating.

It is horrible that these neo-Nazi skinheads attack and murder Turkish women and children, but the root cause of the problem is perhaps not neo-Nazism; it is more likely the German greed and German ambition for profits and markets that made you bring in these workers in the first place, an ambition that you shared with each other and the Turks. You shared it with each other at least insofar as you all approved of and luxuriated in the Wirtschaftswunder. *This huge migration you accepted and encouraged. Even if you did not then realize the risk to your own culture, you clearly have a great responsibility to protect the people who are there. But we are certainly not the ones to lecture you about that. My guess is that the xenophobia of Germany today is far more cultural than economic, and that is exactly the same xenophobia to which Hitler appealed, to which Zhirinovsky is appealing in Russia, and which the aborigines of the Americas understandably feel as they try to preserve the few shards of their remaining culture. Why should the natives of North America be subject to any more of what has already nearly destroyed them? When the Germans look at their immigrants, they feel the same fear and resentment, even if it has far less justification. They say, like the first aborigines, Where will this end? How will it end? It does not matter that the Germans vastly outnumber the foreigners right now, for so did the aborigines of Scotland, Ireland, and North America outnumber the first Anglo-Saxon migrants.*

It seems to me you repeat a common mistake when you refer to people wishing to migrate to a certain place. People migrate for many reasons, chief of which in early North American experience was desire for land or desire for freedom, and nowadays for work, wealth, and sometimes freedom. All of these except land are conditions created by people. Even the land to a great extent is a created condition, i.e., made usable, by the people in possession. For instance, the British, the French, and then the Canadians explored the west for centuries, achieved a political settlement with the natives (however shaky and ill-conceived), and then built the Canadian Pacific Railway, opening the west to farmers. Then it was discovered that the wheats in use at the time did not ripen soon enough, and were often killed off by early frost. So the Canadians developed a type of wheat (Marquis) that ripens earlier than the other wheats, et voilà, the land was useful in a brand-new way. Until all that was done, the land of the Canadian prairie might as well have been part of the Pacific Ocean for all its use to immigrant farmers.

In other words, most people migrate because they prefer the hosts' society to their own. The hosts fear that so many new arrivals will destroy not just the wealth but also the society itself. This fear is justified by history. The original hosts in the Americas, who at first welcomed the newcomers, in the end lost their society and their land. That happened here, and it is what largely happened in Ireland and Scotland. It was well on the way to happening in Africa and India, when finally the local populations expelled the newcomers.

There is only one sure solution to this problem, and that is not to create it in the first place. For immigration without risk, the immigrants and hosts should want to live with each other, like, say, North Europeans now arriving in North America, or German refugees in Germany. The only other condition that counts in modern emigration, it seems to me, is the fine interplay between the need of the migrant and the generosity of the host. Both Canada and Germany have, up to now, a remarkable, maybe even an admirable, record in this regard. It is not to be wondered at that sometimes would-be migrants abuse the generosity of the host by trying to evade the rules, or that the hosts in hard times do not feel as generous as when they were more prosperous.

There is scarcely likely to be racial strife in a country that had no migrants culturally different from the host culture. But for white liberals to blame anyone for not wanting an alien culture set into one's society flies in the face of liberalism itself, which used to decry the imposition of white society on other societies in, say, Africa or India. As soon as they could, the black Africans kicked out their white rulers, the Muslim and Hindu Indians kicked out the British with glee, and everybody today applauds these movements as historically inevitable, a good thing.

Nowadays, people from these same former colonies object if they are not allowed access to the U.K. or Canada, or when Canadians demand that they give up some customs in order to fit in. For this, Canadians today, or Germans who resist immigration of foreign culture, are sneered at as prejudiced. Yet their motives are exactly the same, to preserve a way of life. The Canadians who want their Mounties to go on wearing their famous wide-brimmed hats, not Sikh turbans, are reacting just as Indians did fifty or a hundred years ago when they objected to the spread of British ways and rule in India.

Those who favour immigration in principle are usually saying, We adore multiculturalism; it shows how well we have learned to get on with each other. I am one of those and I have in the past helped to bring many refugees to Canada, but I would not feel nearly as easy about starting that program again now, because although I want to help refugees, I would first want more approval than I now foresee from my fellow citizens before I added to their burdens. I mean not just the taxes, but also, for instance, the burden of teachers trying to cope, as my wife does every day, with a huge influx of immigrant children who cannot speak or write English. Our worries about taxes, social welfare, alien habits, destruction of our culture have overcome some of the generosity we used freely to extend.

Clearly, we need more time and teaching before we take up that light burden again, which in the end gives so much happiness to ourselves and those whom we help.

One of the tragedies of the twentieth century was the horrible experiments in social engineering carried to wild extremes in Europe, which we largely escaped here. But setting immigration quotas beyond the willing welcome of the people is just such a mistake, however well-meant, however mild in comparison to others we have seen.

We have welcomed many people here and doubtless will again, but for the moment the people of this country are saying, Slow down, wait. It is essential to listen to that voice. If we don't, there will be trouble, of roughly the kind that there was in black Africa or brown India when the Europeans were outstaying their dubious welcome.

Your remarks about Lord Byron lamenting the fate of the Greeks under the Turks is apt. And finally the Greeks did defend themselves, with our help, and have since showed themselves as bloody-minded as anyone. (A historical aside here: when Byron stood on the shores of the Hellespont, my ancestors were still arriving in Canada; now my cousin, an army officer whose luxurious cottage is on the family estate, a hundred metres from where I am writing this, has recently returned from keeping the peace between Greeks and Turks in Cyprus. That was in Byron's time an unimaginable mission from a people that did not even exist.)

As for the German neo-Nazis, I don't take them seriously. Every time I might just start worrying about them, I call up something that happened to me a few years ago. It has an element of fantasy about it, but that doesn't detract from its symbolic significance for me. My assistant, Jessica, and I were then travelling in Germany doing research for Other Losses. *In Koblenz we sat in a bar in the evening, drinking and smoking. Three German men noticed Jessica, who was twenty-six, has blond hair, blue eyes, a calm self-possessed air. The Germans got very excited, and one of them came over to ask us to join them. We sat drinking and singing. Jessica pulled out a cigarette. One German snapped his lighter, but another, a handsome, blond Aryan, who looked like a Nazi tank commander from a propaganda poster, leaned forward, rudely blew out his friend's lighter, and struck a whole book of matches at once. He offered the torch to Jessica, who lit her cigarette. That man, so aggressive, so sneering and arrogant, I decided, must be the Fuehrer's Aryan incarnate.*

Then, a few minutes later, when I was coming back upstairs from the men's room on the ground floor, I saw him approaching at the top of the stairs. And as he was standing there, still on the floor, while I was two steps down, my head — I am six feet tall — was level with his. The blond Aryan was hardly bigger than a ten- year-old-boy. In the middle of all that Nazi-ness was a little man who felt inferior.

You see, I had no factual evidence for his being a neo-Nazi. But the encounter taught me not to fear neo-Nazis. Even numerically, they are inferior — your police say they number only around six thousand. If the Germans are serious about dealing with them, as I think they are, they should find it easy to deal with them by routine police work. Recently it was reported here that an exhibition of photos that included one of Hitler by his photographer was found so offensive by the Jews of Berlin that it was banned by the authorities, although it had been on public display in Munich for many weeks without causing offence. Is this report true, and if so, what do you think of it? One hears in Canada that the Germans in school today are taught nothing about their Nazi past. The film Das schreckliche Mädchen *is based entirely on the assumption that for some Germans at least, the Hitler events are dead and buried, never to be discussed, and therefore never to be understood. I cannot understand how it can be that simultaneously the Germans feel the guilt and grief, as you assure me, and at the same time teach almost none of the history, and even suppress it, as we now see with that film and the photographs (if that is true). It seems that the years from 1933 to 1945 are a huge "black hole" in the national historical consciousness and therefore in the German conscience.*

One can see how many Jews would find this display offensive, although surely the Munich reaction offers more hope for the future. What is a bit odd is that the Christian or secular Germans themselves fear this reaction so much that their desire to learn is frustrated. I agree with you 100 per cent that my "philippic" should not discourage all the decent, earnest Germans. But I do not worry much about the Nazis taking heart; even if they were somewhat more numerous, I would not worry much. If lies have been told and it is important that truth be established — which I know is not always the case — then you should blame the liars and deceivers, not me, for the trouble that truth telling may cause.

You think I am a terrible puritan — not so (just ask Elisabeth). But more, I do not think that the easy cannot be good. Only the good is good. You imagine my hitting the Germans with a sledgehammer, but if the truth in Other Losses *is a sledgehammer, remember that all I did was find it. And I do try to retain lightness of spirit and even humour wherever I possibly can. See my final sentence in the letter to the* FAZ *replying to the attack made on me by Prof. Manfred Messerschmidt. ("I have been attacked by a Messerschmidt, but I have not been shot down.") You told me on the phone that you think the* FAZ *saved me embarrassment by refusing to print that sentence, but I have to ask you now, where does the prohibition on fun stop in Germany? An unanswerable question, I know, but I want to point out one thing: it is a very old tradition in the Anglo-Saxon countries, going back at least to Joe Miller's joke book of the seventeenth century to laugh at the discomfiture of the rich and pompous. The most witless pratfall, scarcely funny at all, was thought to become hilarious if one of the characters in it was a duke or a bishop with a famous name and rank.*

You say it is verboten *to make fun of a name, but I did not make fun of a name, I made some fun out of the fact that Professor Messerschmidt's name is the same as the famous airplane, which in no way discredited the professor (or the plane). What I did mock, in high spirits, was the feebleness of the attack. And I think that that is why the* FAZ *refused to print it. They were protecting one of the pillars of German society, a professor.*

The mighty of this world hate humour because it destroys the awe that power largely depends on. For a man like Hitler, or Stalin, to be mocked was dangerous because it destroyed the mystique, bringing him down to the level of the everyday comprehensible. The hero cannot be absurd. The myth cannot withstand the scorn of mockery. I think you can see the truth of this in your own experience, when you were amazed to encounter the cartoons of Bill Mauldin in the U.S. Army newspaper Stars and Stripes, *mocking the army officers. You had never seen anything like that in the Wehrmacht. And that is one of the reasons that there is less tyranny in the West than elsewhere. We have the freedom to laugh.*

You are right about the many German statesmen who were not the cowardly guilt-ridden type. Adenauer spoke out strongly against the crimes in the East. You "tremble somewhat at the rashness" with which I "appear to embrace the number of six million dead..." In the first place, I think it was closer to seven million than to six, and second, I have not yet published that number, so you should tremble at the rashness of Adenauer, who in fact did publish that figure. And indeed, he was much more rash than I, because he accuses the allies of killing off six million persons among only about fifteen million refugees, whereas I say around seven million among sixty million in the whole nation in 1945.

You refer to Adenauer's "assumptions" about six million dead Germans, descending to the pejorative perhaps because you don't know the research work that Adenauer's figures are largely based on. The research was done by Dr. Gustav Stolper, an anti-Nazi member of the Reichstag who fled Germany in the 1930s, went to the U.S., and returned with the Hoover Famine Emergency Commission in 1946. He was appointed by the president of the United States to high rank in the commission headed by a former U.S. president. Not only did Stolper represent great authority, but he also had great authority himself, in his experience, knowledge, and sympathy. He travelled all over Germany with the right to inspect all American military government documents, to copy them, and to bring them home, which he did. He also had the right to interview American army officers and so on. He then published a book on the subject, German Realities. *The report that Hoover issued, based partly on Stolper, was a masterpiece that prompted very important American government action. And Hoover and Stolper were invited back a second time to do similar work in more detail. It was Stolper who first said that six million were dead among the circa fifteen million expellees, a far higher proportion than I say.*

In the Hoover archive, which you inquire about, are hundreds of thousands of pages of documents gathered in Germany by the Hoover commission describing the plight of German civilians under Allied occu-

pation. Among these are a dozen or more documents from, for example, the chief surgeon of the U.S. Army, the medical officer of the U.S. Army in Europe, and from German doctors giving death totals, death rates, and sickness tables for the American-zone civilian population from 1945 onward. All these detailed documents but one report a fantastically high death rate.

The exception is the report sent to the president by the military governor. The death rate he reported is scarcely above the pre-war norm. Further proof of the cover-up by the army and government of the German tragedy appears in the Congressional Record, *reporting speeches by such eminent senators as William Langer and Homer Capehart. These reports describe the senators' own investigations into the horrors being inflicted on the Germans by the Allies. On the basis of these investigations, the senators angrily denounced American policy as vicious, cruel, and wasteful. They denounced the U.S. government propaganda that said that the Morgenthau Plan had been abandoned while in fact it was being implemented. They said the plan was "addlepated and vicious."*

And finally if you don't trust the conqueror's records, consider the report written in the German city of Brilon in 1946 and collected by the Canadian Army, and now on deposit in the National Archives of Canada. The report shows that in the eleven months from May 1945 through April 1946, the death rate in this city more favoured than most in Germany was thirty-four per thousand a year, nearly triple the rate reported by the U.S. military governor. And Brilon was occupied by the British and Canadians, who were treating the Germans far too softly, according to U.S. Army general Hilldring.

And what do we find in the German Federal government records today? (Remember my last letter?) For the Hungerjahr *1947 they virtually report the same death rate as appears in the military governor reports, which is fewer than in prosperous West Germany in 1968. We have to wonder how it can be that this egregious and important impossibility has been presented as fact for over four decades? Can it be a mistake? Can it be anything but a lie? If so, it must have been invented and then widely accepted only because it helped to blind people to terrible truths. Yet at the same time, the Germans have been able to accept the terrible responsibility for their atrocities toward all kinds of innocent people.*

This is a result of my research, but I have done nothing that the Bonn government could not have done forty years since, if they had had the gumption. The two most important elements of the discovery above have been available for many years. All it required was a willing suspension of belief *to find out the facts. Nor can the Canadian, British, and American soldiers who gathered these figures in 1945 be accused of revisionism. All the figures showing Allied atrocities were solemnly reported by a conquering army about as close to Nazism as you are to a Plains Cree buffalo hunter. You see, all I am doing is exercising common sense in the ideal of liberty provided me by martyrs in our history, an ideal that was supposedly an essential force driving our men forward against Herr Adolf Grosslüge himself.*

J.

April 24, 1994

Dear Jim,

The week after Easter I had to go to the clinic in Aachen to get my prostate "shelled out." At the clinic as a habit of a lifetime I kept my nerve by reading my favourite weekly: good old *New Statesman*, in almost any position, even on the operating table, and by reading two novels as worlds apart as Trollope's *Barchester Towers* and Kenneally's *Schindler's Ark* (or *List*, as it is now called). What novelist's craftsmanship in shrugged-off Trollope, whom I had never before bothered to read! And then, Oskar Schindler. How in a way his novel reminded me of your Laporterie — and who has the film options on his story? I greatly admire Spielberg's as well as Kenneally's achievement. Between them they have managed to succeed where all former attempts at "Holocaust" failed. They discovered the rhetoric, didactic, i.e., poetic means to open a passage through the natural defences of the human psyche for the abysmal subject — vaguely comparable to what Shakespearean and Greek tragedy did.

It's mere abstraction and intellectual wrongheadedness to say that Spielberg and all that "Hollywood" in his film interpose themselves between us and the awful anonymity of the real thing. It's true, of course. But as you cannot see anything in the world but under the conditions set by the laws of your eye, so the "real thing of horror" cannot enter your soul but under the laws of the human heart. And that demands something very strong and reassuring before it will allow anything like the true horror to enter. Schindler, the real one, making the book and the film possible, did unwittingly more than save the lives of thirteen hundred Jews.

But instead of rejoicing at the film and its impact in Germany, the professional castigators, mean-minded as they believe it their duty to be, cry halt. Don't you Germans feel any psychic uplift from this (as genuine art entails). Don't dare soar with Schindler, not even you fifty or so million younger ones who couldn't possibly be guilty of the Holocaust. For you and your guilty forebears, Oskar is not to be anything but hard proof of what could and should have been done under the Nazis — giving the lie to all the whining excuses for German passivity and collaboration. There!

But if anything, film and book make us realize what miraculously improbable conditions besides compassion for the victims and hate of Nazi crime were essential to pull off such a trick. How I love the bon vivant and cunning daredevil who risked his life ever so often for nothing but the good cause. Yet how I hate the armchair preachers ticking the other Germans off for not having risked their lives the same way! Although, and thank God really, precious few got into anything like even a starting position to attempt it, let alone a chance of succeeding. See the SS men committing suicide in the face of what was expected of them, see poor *wacht-meister* Bosco at the gates of the Cracow Ghetto putting up all kinds of clandestine resistance to his superiors, and then having to escape to the Polish partisans who shot him, mistaking him for a "traitor."

You have difficulty squaring the pictures offered of today's Germans. You don't know which to believe is true: the mean, distrustful, wilfully blind and shutter-down Germans of the film *Das schreckliche Mädchen* or the Germans having come round to accepting German guilt, confessing it, and making amends (apart from a third image of the Germans reviving Nazi practices or condoning them in secret).

Basically, your plight is of a pretty general nature. From time to time everyone ought to check what his generalizations regarding whole nations are worth in terms of reality. For convenience' sake, one talks of We, of Them, of You (plural), as if they were giant individuals to be fairly reliably observed, characterized, and assessed at a glance.

But often we get a fuller bucket of reality by recognizing two or more Canadas, Americas, Russias, and Germanys. Take the question of inviting immigrants and then resenting their staying on. It's true, the first Turkish million didn't arrive in Germany of their own accord; they were incited to come here. That, you say, was "Germany" — greedy for the *Wirtschaftswunder.* But more than 99 per cent of Germans can truly say, "We? Invite Turks? Surely nobody asked *us.*" Those clamouring for "guest workers" (and for nothing more permanent than guests, as even the Turks themselves and the Turkish government insisted in those days) were of course the managers of the mines and steel plants at the Ruhr, the big car manufacturers, etc. This was when the reinvestment of the big money those firms had made in the decade before and the deployment of ready capital from abroad were hampered merely by a recent lack of (cheap enough) labour. The *wunder* part of the *Wirtschaftswunder* was well over then, fired as it had been by great home demand and a big surplus workforce of German expellees from the East. By now it was a question of keeping up growth — in sales terms: of export. "The" Germans, especially the German workers and their unions, were anything but enthusiastic about guest workers. And when the day arrived that these Turks were to go back to Turkey in order not to lose their native roots and help with developing their home country (and other Turks having been earmarked to take their turn in Germany), who called on the two governments to keep the first million in Germany? It was the big bosses again, wanting their investment in human capital to pay further dividends, not "the" Germans. After all, this country is no Canada, no U.S., no Russia. It was then, and still is, one of the most overpopulated countries in the world, not really viable in ecological terms, not even if the population shrinks as dramatically as the demographs calculate for the next century.

But then, this question of "Who's We" with regard to immigration policy is really an old one. The traditionally large German populations inside Russia, Romania, Hungary, the Baltic, and Poland, when persecuted as unwelcome foreigners during the last war and after, could rightly point out that their ancestors hadn't forced themselves on these parts but had responded to urgent calls of the princes ruling those countries who lacked qualified subjects to turn the natural resources of their lands into taxable wealth. The Russian peasants were never asked whether they welcomed their model neighbours of a different language and religion, running their farms more efficiently than they. And who are "the" Americans you mention, keen on defending their country in Europe? How long did it take tricky Roosevelt to make them go and die for America — and only with massive help from the Japanese and Hitler into the bargain! Not even "the" Germans can be said to have started the Second World War. Hitler had to use a con trick (having SS men in Polish uniforms cross the border to Germany and blow up Gleiwitz radio station) in order to convince a deeply reluctant people that war was again inevitable.

Who again is "we," "the" Germans failing to live up to the challenge of young idealists like the Nasty Girl trying to discover and come to terms with the secrets of their Nazi days? Is it "us," or only a small and negligible minority? And if it is not a negligible minority, does that put paid to the German claim of having fundamentally changed for the better? In my dialogues *On Germany*, my first political book, published in 1965, I presumed that the thickheaded ones were in fact still the majority, although I let a "son" speak for them; also that it was premature to claim that Germany had changed fundamentally. I went into the fray with a lot of artistic and political acumen, and to my and everybody's surprise met with a huge national echo, overwhelmingly positive. It was as if I had found a wellspring nobody had known existed. It surely was a success story, short-lived only in the sense that a little later the student revolution took over, burying anything less radical or less Marxist. So today it's common to say that it was the students of '68 who for the first time brought the nation face to face with its Nazi past.

But no matter: whatever the origin or the form, the condemnation and self-condemnation of more and more facets of the German past got well under way: not the Wehrmacht or the churches or the judiciary or the universities were spared any longer. The aggressively anti-fascist spirit took hold of the commanding heights, especially in the media, days of remembrance and contrition were instituted, monuments erected, streets renamed, former concentration camps salvaged, synagogues rebuilt, speeches made. Willy Brandt fell on his knees in Warsaw. Jewish officials, arriving from America in the late 1980s, were taken aback at the "cult of contrition" they found had sprung up all over Germany: no more hushing up of the Nazi past. On the contrary, reidentification of a nation via its sins. This, I should think, testifies well to the picture I'm drawing, especially because these Jewish leaders, though acknowledging that much, were far from liking what they saw: the horrors of the Holocaust midwifing a new German unity and nationalism? Elated, carefree penitents? They decided that the hurdles for reconciliation and a new Germany's final acceptance in the civilized world had better be raised by another couple of inches.

The trouble is that meanwhile this German movement of atonement and change of heart, which for all practical purposes has become the German establishment, got drunk on its wonderful morality and began to lose all sense of reality. The more general and undisputed their position became, the more hectoring their tone, the less tolerant they grew toward any sign of even the most legitimate and common-sensical criticism. Anything not moving exactly on the prescribed rails of repentance was immediately denounced as Nazism raising its ugly head again. In short, all the symptoms of totalitarianism and its paranoia, well established in communist countries, are now theirs. A short respite occurred when in 1989 the communist world went to pieces, but the subsequent emergence of the "foreigners question" and the terrorism of the Right propped them up again. Consequently, liberalism, the only anti-Nazi position that ever convinced *me*, is in deep trouble in Germany now, not at the hands of the neo-Nazis but at the hands of those fighting them: my old friends of the '60s.

Are you with me, Jim, if I say that I couldn't but defect from their camp if I was to remain true to my deeper self? It's probably the stupidity of *any* victorious movement that will drive me into relative opposition.

I began to sympathize with the obstinate Germans being flailed on every public TV channel at least once a week, and more often than that in *Die Zeit* and other quality papers. What, I began telling myself, could be more normal than people not very much liking their inglorious past being raked up! In contrast to us masters of political correctness or your beady-eyed teenage researcher, what kicks were they supposed to get out of it? How could the moralists preaching down at them ever forget another, more ancient system of ethics: the duties of shielding the family name, of protecting your parents and forebears, your friends, your nation if attacked. For surely "My country, right or wrong," with whatever natural ties are meant by "country," has not yet completely vanished from the world of common decency. Or has it? Remember the Fourth Commandment? And what about the teasing nature of those janus words *collaboration* and *denunciation*, depending for their moral status on all sorts of heart-rending distinctions?

Mind, I'm not at all advocating this traditional normality — neither in principle nor by natural inclination. I believe in the necessity of objective justice. I am on the side of a higher morality than clannishness to provide for today's world and its future. But for heaven's sake, let's acknowledge the difficulty of such objectivity for most people in the world who would rather not rise above their own or their family's or their village's or their nation's immediate interests.

Too many people judging Germans, including German critics of Germany, have by now lost their common sense, their heads, even, to the effect of creating a fictitious world of universal morality with almost no resemblance to the world as it is. This is unfairly hard on a large portion of any people. What is more, it positively damages the chances of leading them out of their shells or, for that matter, of educating a large body of very young Germans who have simply stopped listening to Nanny any longer.

To answer your question: yes, there are, I suppose, a considerable number of older Germans, guilty at least by association, and there are some younger ones, doggedly refusing to rally to the call for remembrance and repentance. Which, however, I insist, is only natural. Voluntary repentance in individuals, let alone collectively, exists as a text for pious sermons, as a moral demand, as wishful thinking, but hardly as a reality anywhere — *except Germany*. As you readily confirm, "we" are unique in world history to have nationally embraced contrition and atonement. Isn't it about time somebody started praising and respecting us for it?

To be sure, I blush at this tactless remark of mine. My only excuse for unsavourily extolling German virtue is just the faintest of hopes that someone somewhere out there might honestly wish to keep us at it.

Those Germans refusing to climb the higher rungs of morality, preferring the path natural to the guilty of this world I think had best be left alone; unless, that is, one really cared for them and had a loving way of showing them the light.

For understandable but nevertheless irrational reasons, the victims of Nazism and their friends find this position unacceptable. In their eyes, Germany, almost by definition, cannot be right, let alone be a model to others. When I accuse these people of using double standards, they contend that the enormity of German guilt warrants any excess of penance to be demanded of them. But that's a mistaken notion. If greater crimes naturally made for greater inclination toward contrition, the argument might just hold. But there is not the slightest evidence of this. The reverse is nearer the truth. What the argument does justify is the victims' and the victims' friends' determination not to let these Krauts ever have the upper hand again, not even morality-wise. But that's nothing to do with what we are talking about.

Your second question was, Do they (or do they not) teach about the Third Reich in German schools? The answer is, Yes, they do teach about Hitler and the Holocaust in schools. The immediate after-war years were different, but for at least thirty years now, that period has had a high priority in the curricula, and one might even argue disproportionately so. But as is so often the case when people get worked up about a subject, they have difficulty using their brains. Teaching, alas, is not equivalent to learning. Some people learn almost nothing in school, and most learn far, far less than teachers can allow themselves to admit. Many boys and girls simply can't be bothered to take the slightest interest in certain subjects or certain teachers; everybody has plenty of evidence for this. And yet everybody cries out for more school and "more of the same" when some particular scandal of ignorance surfaces. It's hard to take seriously.

The truth about the place of the Third Reich in schools is that history lessons in general have been cut to the advantage of other subjects, mainly at the instigation of the '68 reformers; also that serious history is no great favourite with young people anyway, who prefer computers, dinosaurs, astrophysics, and ecology, for all I know. And then it takes a damn good teacher to overcome the natural tedium or aversion to subjects suspected of being politically pushed. Most teachers are not damn good, and thus their engagement about the Third Reich may indeed leave something to be desired. In my time as teacher I made the Third Reich a great issue. Not being a history teacher, I did it in German and English classes, which was in fact easier. And of course I had the particular advantage of novelty in 1960 and thereafter.

The whole thing reminds me sadly of all those hundreds of thousands of lessons of Marxist philosophy (and of Russian language too) that were compulsory in the GDR, and to almost no visible effect. *Schindler's List*, both the novel and the movie, will do for a generation of young Germans more than any compulsory teaching of that depressing subject could ever hope to achieve. And what about that (non-)exhibition of Hitler photos in Munich and Berlin?

Well, it's one of those things one gets sadly tired of thinking about. All was set for the opening of the well-wrought exhibition, when the chairman of the Berlin Jewish community approached the man in charge and asked very softly, Couldn't Berlin abstain? He wouldn't kick up a row if they didn't; it was not a demand, just a question. But it would be so hard on the memories of the Jews of Berlin.

Well, wouldn't even I or you have been moved? You may be right that the Nazis in Germany are no threat once we recognize what a sorry lot they really are. But the trouble is that Turks or Ghaneans killed, synagogues or Jewish gravestones defaced, however common in a world of vandalism and violent deaths such things may be, are our German deaths and horrors just the same. And while the famous terrorism of the Left in the '70s was an underground affair of a tightly knit group of adults, directing their homicidal energies at a distinct elite of VIPs, it's much more difficult for the state and its police to respond adequately to every youngster itching to do something conspicuously bad in any of the hundreds of towns of this country. If such a boy wants that particular kick of being talked about by drawn and shocked faces on TV, there aren't, after all, many taboos left for him to trespass. The fire bombing should of course never have started, should never have gathered the momentum it has. But such is history: never at a loss for springing a new dilemma on some society.

Still, for me the steps to be taken are quite clear: as far as is sensible and possible, remove on the quiet all valid excuses for the crimes committed but come down really hard on the perpetrators. Be careful not to confuse opinions to be tolerated, however distasteful, with actions that are not. Do not by indiscriminate accusations and imputations increase the forces of the enemy, driving the wavering or naive into the wrong camp. And so on. Anybody with any experience of unruly school classes, neighbourhood gangs or, for that matter, deserting troops, knows that once the fat's in the fire, only sophisticated double strategies have a chance of containing the damage and reversing the direction of events.

You are of course quite right, and I couldn't agree more, that we should undertake every measure in our power to make this country safe for the foreigners forming a legal part of our polity and society, no matter how many they are and even if with hindsight we might prefer not to have admitted them in the first place. But in my mind it's pure unreasonableness and demagogy to say that that objective calls for the unhampered and indiscriminate admittance of ever further millions of foreigners. Yet that appears to be the accepted doctrine of the good and progressive people in Germany. If you doubt its wisdom, you are denounced as an enemy of democracy, of Germany's foreigners, a supporter of Nazi bomb throwers. Now, how does that strike you?

Well, Jim, there is still the Messerschmidt joke you insist should not have been cut from your letter to the *FAZ.* But as I told you, it doesn't come off grammatically well enough (in German!) for the uneasiness about playing with someone's proper name to be quelled. And then, of course, though Messerschmidt wrote a poor enough article, showing up the German professors for the poodles to the U.S. that they are, you cannot but be aware that he was referring to some more serious research being done in America, published by Günter Bischof and Stephen E. Ambrose in *Eisenhower and the German POWs* (1992). Why court nemesis by cracking gratuitous jokes at their little minion? Of course there is still a lot of simply partisan trash and circumventing of facts in that book. But I must confess that I was impressed by Ambrose's defence of Eisenhower. I got the feeling that he is a serious and competent researcher, after all. Yet even if 100 per cent right, he doesn't really undermine your position. Everything you concluded to have originated with Eisenhower must in his view be laid at the door of people higher up the ladder, including Roosevelt. He and Bischof obviously don't realize how severely this defence diminishes the status of their hero, putting him structurally and characterwise in the shoes of Field Marshall Keitel ("Lakei-tel").[17] When charged with war crimes, he had also done nothing but obeyed orders.

R.

---

17 Generalfeldmarschall Wilhelm Keitel (*1882), 1938 Chief of the High Command of the *Wehrmacht.* Devoted to Hitler. On 8th May 1945 he signed the capitulation on the Eastern Front. Hanged in Nuremberg 1946. The nick-name *Lakeitel,* which he was given behind his back, is a conflation of his name "Keitel" with the word *Lakai,* meaning "lackey" (to Hitler).

Müller was "Flakhilfer," or assistant air defence gunner in 1943.

In 1946, Bacque attained the rank of lance corporal, in the Upper Canada College Cadet Battalion, Toronto.
U.C.C. Archives.

Bacque (right) with his younger brother Gordon and their mother, Edith, at their house in Moore Park, Toronto, spring circa 1941.

Müller with his dog Senta in 1940.

Elizabeth Bacque
with King George
VI, inspects
members of her
command at their
Royal Canadian
Air Force Base,
No. 6 Bomber
Group, North
Allerton, in York-
shire, England,
1944.

Müller (front
left) with com-
rades in front of
Cologne Cathe-
dral, August 1943
as they changed
trains enroute to
flak shooting
range near
Monschau.

Müller as a teacher in Cologne, in the mid-sixties.

Bacque was writing a novel at his house in Toronto about 1979.

Bacque and Müller pose for this book at Müller's country house near
Monschau, autumn 1996.

Frederic Bacque and Edith (seated) with their children, Gordon,
Elizabeth, Hugh, Graeme and James. At Georgian Bay, probably 1941.

July 3, 1994

Dear Richard,

While you, dear boy of seventeen, were forming up into the Wehrmacht with your machine gun on your skinny shoulder, I was lying here on the dock at the cottage sunning myself and watching to the east the freighters come and go with wheat, lumber, munitions, the warships going out painted grey to make war on you. Against that east sky, today so purely blue around the white-and-purple clouds, there streamed out from warship and freighter long banners of black smoke, which I imagined to be the smoke from the fires of London and Berlin.

The smoke from Germany was caused partly by Canadian raids planned by my sister, who was then in charge of the women's division of the Royal Canadian Air Force at a big Canadian base in Yorkshire. I was proud of her then and for long after, and in a way, I still am. But something else sprang up in me when I stood in the square of a Rhine city on the bronze plaque placed in memory of the air raid that destroyed it. I was standing right over that plaque without even noticing it; I did not notice it until an English visitor showed it to me, and read it for me. For a brief dizzying moment standing high over it unnoticing, I was just like the pilots far above this city on that day, loosing tons of destruction on people they did not see below them.

My sister was a hero, all my family fighting you were heroes.

The war, after all, was caused 100 per cent by you and won 100 per cent by us. So you bear all the guilt while we feel only the weight of the laurels round our brows. The celebrations at D Day a few weeks ago, in which Germans were forbidden to share, proved this all over again.

Nor is this remote from me here today. A few hours ago, I saved my cousin's boat from the rocks in front of this cottage: he was an officer in a Canadian regiment that helped to beat the Wehrmacht in Italy and then in Holland. Another relative of mine not fifty metres from here cleared the way to shore for the fleets of D Day. Yes, we marched from victory to victory in those days. And we still do. But I can no longer celebrate it. I think the unthinkable thoughts, such as, Hoover said we should not fight the Soviets but wait for them to fall apart, which was inevitable, because the system could not work. And he was right. We have seen his prediction come true. So then I think, What if we had simply armed ourselves in 1939, and then waited for Hitler to die? He would have conquered the

U.S.S.R., but most likely he would have soon been overthrown by Germans. And in any case, he would certainly have died by now. Either way, Germany would have come to its senses, just like Russia. It is no answer to say that most of Europe and all the U.S.S.R. would have been enslaved by the fascists, for most of these people were enslaved anyway, by communists. At the very least, if we had not declared war on Hitler, and if we had left the U.S.S.R. to fight him alone, many millions of lives would have been saved.

This is why your long panegyric to Schindler's List *left me unmoved. It seems to me that you express something commonly felt around all the English- and French-speaking democracies when you refer to the "miraculously improbable conditions" that were essential to pull off such a trick as saving those persecuted Jews. What's commonly believed in the Western democracies is that Germany was so strongly united behind Hitler that we had to impose Unconditional Surrender on you, because there were no good Germans to treat with.*

Don't you know how many Germans resisted Hitler? There were over 600,000 who were actually caught and imprisoned. Think how many more helped them, or countenanced their behaviour, or resisted but were not caught. Think of the names — the most famous general, Erwin Rommel, the head of the spy service, Adm. Wilhelm Canaris, the number-two Nazi Party leader, Rudolf Hess, the aristocrats like Claus von Stauffenberg, the generals and field marshals like Beck, the clergymen like Martin Niemöller, the politicians, businessmen, teachers, students, all making up the only serious national resistance movement of any size in the whole war, apart from the special case of the Ukrainian and Baltic freedom fighters in the U.S.S.R. Only Germans made serious attempts to assassinate their national leader. Thousands and thousands of them were caught and executed for their attempts to rid their country and the world of the Hitler scourge. Yet today in Germany these people are scarcely remembered, books about them are rare and not much read, there has never been, to my knowledge, a film or play or big TV series glorifying their supreme sacrifices.

You call me a puritan for my moralizing about your failure to denounce our lies and atrocities against you. You praise Schindler, who after all affected the lives of so few people, while the work of the Kreisau Circle, Canaris, the White Rose, die Rote Kapelle[18] and many others

---

18 *Kreisau Circle*: Civilian resisters meeting regularly at Kreisau, home of Graf Helmuth James von Moltke, from 1940 onwards. Many executed in 1944. - Admiral Wilhelm Canaris, Chief of the German Military Intelligence,

certainly helped the Allied war effort, saving possibly many thousands of lives. The disorganization on Eastern and Western fronts caused by Stülpnagel,[19] Canaris, Rommel, Beck, von Stauffenberg, and the hundreds of others in the July 1944 plot alone certainly made it easier for both Russians and ourselves to advance. Where is the honour due those heroes? Forgotten, all forgotten, and their deeds along with them. To your shame. I think it is at least a tenable thesis that your president, Richard von Weizsäcker, is the only important German government figure today to attack remorselessly the atrocities of the neo-Nazis, because he is also the only one descended from a resistance hero, his father, Ernst von Weizsäcker, who struggled against Hitler from 1938. Here I suppose is the heart of my objection to the German attitude today — your contrition is sentimental, because it is all a matter of superficial feeling easily forgotten, a debt payable to some degree in cash, whereas the resistance heroes you had in greater abundance than any nation except possibly the U.S.S.R. have taught you no lesson at all. If German contrition were really true, surely you would honour these heroes because they represented at least a heroic anti-Nazism, as well as an honourable pro-Germanism. And some of them, like the Kreisau Circle, were among the bravest, most compassionate Christian democrats in the world for many, many years. That "the" Germans neglect these people seems to me a sign that the conversion of the Germans is less than sincere. And I suggest that this is because it is almost impossible even for young Germans today to avoid the thought that these men were technically traitors. So nationalism still triumphs over the higher moral ideals that these resistance heroes embodied, and died for.

The Globe and Mail *has just reported (August 29, 1994) from Luckenwalde, Germany, in the former eastern zone, that many "Ossis" feel a longing for their communist past. This gives rise to fears of a*

---

provided the German resistance with information and cover, helped Jews, was arrested in 1944 and executed in a concentration camp, shortly before it was liberated by US troops. — *The White Rose:* Munich resistance group around the students Hans and Sophie Scholz from 1942 onwards, most of them executed in 1943. — *Rote Kapelle:* Secret-police name for a mainly communist espionage and sabotage group 1938-1942, originally operating in countries around Germany, then in Germany itself. In 1942 six hundred suspects were arrested, about 50 executed.

19 General Karl-Heinrich von Stülpnagel, friend of Ludwig Beck, leading figure in the resistance. On the 20th July 1944 he took 1200 SS and Secret Police prisoner in Paris. Condemned to death and executed.

resurgent communism, just like the fears of a resurgent Nazism. The Ossis apparently miss the former certitudes. This is not just a hankering for the artifacts and atmosphere and feelings and fun of their youth. This new feeling cannot be that sentimental longing of the middle-aged for their lost youth, because only three years have passed since the regime fell and because they are not so much hankering after artifacts and memories but are actually honouring the past with, for example, free admission tickets to concerts and parties at universities and nightclubs for anyone wearing the blue blouse of the former communist party youth movements. They actually miss communism. This is truly nostalgie de la boue, *and it seems to me that it is just as significant and dangerous as the neo-Nazi movement.*

After all, communism was even more dangerous than Nazism, because it preached hatred and destruction of whole classes of people around the world for advocating self-improvement and ownership of land. Just like Nazi racism, it sought social improvement through eugenic cleansing and lethal camps, and it is a threat to billions of people even today, whereas Nazism has been dead and unmourned for generations. But Nazism in North America is still such a bugaboo that it is cynically used by government as an excuse to extend government's surveillance and coercion over the citizenry.

One of our spy agencies was revealed in 1994 to have actually set up a neo-Nazi race-hate group. Their agent, Grant Bristow, has recently been exposed by a reporter for the Toronto Sun *as the chief builder of the Heritage Front, a purportedly neo-Nazi white supremacist group. The government spies now pretend that he was simply infiltrating the system, but it is clear that there was no neo-Nazi movement of any size or importance until Bristow came along and used taxpayers' money, government-supplied spy "expertise" and police protection to build a network where there had been none before.*

All this the government agency did to expand their activities and budget, to create a shadow enemy they could then attack. Such is the threat of neo-Nazi racism in Canada, which our government pretends is so dangerous that the police were ordered to arrest the revisionist historian David Irving and throw him out of the country in handcuffs. This was not for advocating violence, apparently, but for his controversial historical opinions on the Holocaust. One arm of government finds so little Nazism that it has to help promote it, but the other finds so much that it has to deprive a writer of his civil liberties. A letter of protest signed by Alfred de Zayas and me was refused by the Toronto Star *and by the*

Globe and Mail, *although the* Globe *did print one letter signed by Prof. Jack Granatstein. Apart from this, no one else said a word. There was hardly a peep of protest in the country.*

There is no significant racist movement in Canada, but there is far too much government. And one suspects that much the same thing is going on in Germany. For instance, about a year ago, a German girl in a wheelchair was reported to have been assaulted by neo-Nazis who carved a swastika in her cheek. This story lasted for only a few weeks, until it was revealed, how I do not know, that she was mentally disturbed, had no swastika on her face, had never been assaulted by any Nazis, neo or otherwise, and needed a lot of protection not from Nazis but from herself. I have no doubt at all that we are soon going to be reading wild tales like that of Grant Bristow about German ex-government agents telling how they built a neo-Nazi hate group in order to expose it for a promotion.

You are not experiencing so much a neo-Nazi resurgence as a violent, racist, and undemocratic reaction against unemployment and high taxes. It is an understandable despair among underemployed people venting their frustrations on innocent people. Nazis or communists may exploit these feelings, but the feelings themselves are common everywhere; they are not communist or Nazi in themselves. To apply the label communist or neo-Nazi to these people is to make it easier to ignore the real problems that they are illegally and cruelly trying to eradicate. What is required is not labels that do not fit but policies that work.

The resurgence of German pride is not the same as the return of Nazism, even in my nightmares. We people west of the German border, and our lackeys in your country, are trying to scare everyone with these ancient bugaboos in order to keep Germany under control.

Surely it is significant that in our discussion it is I who has to point out how both our governments exaggerate the Nazi threat and refuse to honour the German resistance. And you — who know the names of Stauffenberg and Niemöller as well as I — ignore these true German heroes entirely while you discuss at length German crimes and guilts, and the difficulty of bearing them. You will do this much more easily if you do not have to feel that all the virtue of that war lay with us, that because you were 100 per cent bad, you then must import all your virtue from us. You know perfectly well that we have none to spare.

When I generalized about "the" Germans and "the" British or Canadians, you rightly asked, "Who are `the' Germans," and offered some rhetorical puzzles that show how hard it is to give a sensible answer — in other words, to define those who committed the crimes. Well, my answer is

*simple. "The" Germans are those German-speaking soldiers of the
Wehrmacht who crossed the border into Poland in 1939, or who paid
their wages in taxes, or who built the army that carried them, or who
cheered them when they "won." "The" Germans are all those who enslaved and killed millions of people. "The" Germans are also the ones
who died under Allied wings in 1944, or who supported the regime
throughout the war, plus those who risked their lives to oppose the regime.
And I could make the same sort of definition for the British, Americans,
and Canadians. Except I would not be able to include any resistors on
our side.*

*Since we are discussing collectives here, and since one of the character-
istics of a member of a collectivity is that he/she follows the leader/
government/ruler of the collectivity, we see right away that "the" Germans
are those who followed Hitler and his government, and the British were
those who followed Churchill, and so on. (It is a strange paradox of the
struggle between Democracy and Totalitarianism that Hitler was elected
to govern, and Churchill was not — except by vote of the House of
Commons).*

*So I do not accept your cavil, which I think obscures the point. Such a
definition would count mainly on some day of reckoning. It is usually
when blame is searching for somewhere to land that fog closes in over the
landscape.*

*Which leads me to a dangerous theory. First, it is indisputable that
large numbers of Germans approved of Hitler, including many people
who were more or less aware that he was probably a dangerous xenophobic
racist. It is also beyond dispute now, according to research conducted by
the very distinguished American writer Dr. Alfred de Zayas that the great
majority of Germans had no idea that Hitler was deliberately exterminat-
ing people because of supposed defects in their physique, character, racial
background, or national origin.*

*It is also clear that one of the things that many Germans knew and
approved in him was his intention to correct the wrongs done to Germany
by the Allies in 1918 to 1921. The collectivity of Germans for whom he
acted included you for a while, and I would bet my bottom dollar that you
knew nothing of the concentration camps, of extermination policy, and
that in the beginning at any rate, you approved Hitler's attempts to
improve the lot of the German people. And why? Because you felt a sense
of kinship with them, you felt the love of land and people called patriotism. In other words, you felt a love of Germany and Germans. And this
love was appealed to by Hitler. It was used and abused, it was warped, it*

was cynically distorted, but that is what it was, among Germans.
Deutschland, Deutschland, über alles, *indeed. And how could such
a sentiment have existed? Easily, I say, among the people who had given
birth to Gutenberg, the Reformation, the art and education of Charlemagne,
Dürer, Holbein, Bach, Mozart, Beethoven, Schiller, Heine, Goethe, Leibniz,
Einstein, and so on and on.*

*Germans were among the most civilized people on earth for a long, long
time, civilized in the sense that they valued the peaceful fruits of life
ahead of everything else. Their natural self-love, so deeply justified, was
easily distorted, and this is what frightens some people who have experience of Germany, including me. I have experienced and hated English
arrogance, the petty French variety, the crude American variety, and I
hate and fear the prospect of a mighty Germany trying to lord it over the
world again, more than almost anything.*

*This patriotism, so scandalously abused by Hitler to gain power, was
clearly also what motivated all the resistance fighters, especially those
whom the Allies first ignored, then denounced. And it was also present in
those who actually rose above it to a supreme Christian view, such as the
resistance hero Helmuth James von Moltke, Stauffenberg, and Pastor
Niemöller. But in the post-war period, the heroes of Germany have not
been these men; the heroes have mainly been the agile politicians like
Willy Brandt who survived Hitler in exile, or the businessmen who presided over the* Wirtschaftswunder *as it enriched them along with the
country. And of course there have been the restored Nazis both in government and in business, who may not have been treated as heroes but were
not condemned as villains.*

*Germans, it seems to me, have not so much reformed themselves as
conformed to the conquerors. In Berlin today there is a Lucius Clay Allee
to honour an Allied conqueror, but probably no Stauffenberg Strasse.
Surely if you really repudiated Hitler, you would honour the men and
principles who attacked him in the name of Germany. But no, you honour
the conqueror. In all honesty, I have to conclude with something really
horrible, for which I am sure you will forgive me, because I know it is not
true of you and your friends and family. What I am talking about is the
old saying still sometimes heard in the West that "the" German is either at
your throat or at your feet. And at the moment it seems that the Germans
are still at our feet.*

*You also referred, in your last letter, to the book concocted by Ambrose
and Bischof to show me wrong. You said that you were impressed by what
seemed to you to be serious and competent research. Oh dear. I am afraid*

you have been deceived by two of the flightless swans of academe who have done no research at all, but simply interpret or misinterpret the work of others. For instance, they give the wrong capture figure for prisoners in American camps. It is low by millions. And where do they get this low, low figure? From a series of tainted books written by an ex-Nazi to exculpate the Americans. This purpose was evasively admitted in the Bundestag by a cabinet minister. But the real capture figures were available to them in reports by the U.S. Army in the U.S. National Archives, which were discovered and used by Col. Dr. Ernest F. Fisher and me in preparing Other Losses. Dr. Fisher is a U.S. Army historian who has no doubt that the documents we used were the only authentic ones on the subject. And why do they need this low figure? The fewer the prisoners, the fewer the likely number of deaths among them.

Swans Ambrose and Bischof say that most of the missing prisoners must have died in Russia, because that is where they were last seen alive. They cite as a source a report from Dr. Margarethe Bitter of Munich. But Dr. Bitter told me on tape in front of a witness, "We did not know where the prisoners were."

Although the Soviet figures have now been published, showing the Ambrose-Bischof book to be in error, neither of them has had the courage to admit they were wrong. In fact they go on repeating their error.[20]

Let us observe one of these flightless swans as he floats about the grove of academe avoiding the issues. Swan Bischof contends that the camp at Ebensee, Austria, was not a prisoner-of-war camp as I say in Other Losses. *He says it was a camp for displaced persons. Bischof boasts of his extensive research, but it has left him extensively ignorant of the evidence showing that Ebensee was a U.S. Army prison camp housing dozens of thousands of prisoners of war in 1945. The evidence is as follows: Gen. Mark Clark's secret report of August 1945 (in the Clark archive at the Citadel in Charleston, South Carolina) about the condition of prisoners of war in the camp, U.S. Army medical reports from the National Archives in Washington, by Lt. Col. Herbert Pollack, describing the starved condition of prisoners in the camp in September 1945, plus an eyewitness account of the catastrophe among thousands of prisoners in a handwritten diary kept by the priest Franz Loidl who ministered to the dying prisoners at Ebensee in the summer of 1945. This manuscript is on*

---

20 Details and sources for these statements are given in James Bacque, *Crimes and Mercies*, London and Toronto: Little, Brown, 1998, 76 et seq.

deposit in the Church History Institute of the Catholic Theological Faculty, University of Vienna.

Furthermore, I have received letters from eyewitnesses who survived that dreadful camp at Ebensee, two ex-prisoners, Al Porsche and Dr. Rudolf Pillwein, both from Pennsylvania. The evidence from Al Porsche will suffice here. Porsche wrote to Bischof on February 8, 1993, saying that Bischof's article was "incorrect," and that Ebensee had indeed housed many thousands of prisoners of war, of whom he was one.

Swan Bischof wrote back to Porsche on February 24, 1993, a friendly letter thanking him, and adding that the information on Ebensee was "highly interesting and I thank you for your corrections." Bischof said that he would "research this matter more deeply and if I made a mistake I'd be the first one to admit and correct it. That's how historical knowledge evolves."

Bischof got his chance to correct his error when I twitted him about this in the Times Literary Supplement *in 1994, but there was no response from him. Historical knowledge has indeed evolved, as he said it does, and it would be a service to his readers to correct the false impression he has created, as he said he would. He has not done this. If that is because he knows he had so few readers that it wasn't worth the trouble, I have done it for him here.*

Not only on this subject does Bischof get it wrong, but also on my interviews with Col. Lauben and a guard named Johnny Foster. As well as Bischof, other swans in the book are making a pointless flap. The statistics on food are wrong, the very important Eisenhower order forbidding German civilians to feed prisoners on pain of death is missing, and so on.

These are only a few of many examples of the kind of errors in the book. T'were boring to rehearse them all here before you.

Damn. I wish I had never started this series of letters with you. It makes me feel so sad. And so mixed. I can hardly believe that my pessimistic view of Germany today is accurate, and yet I cannot see how you can prove it otherwise.

Auf Wiedersehen

J.

P.S. A bolt out of the blue. Yesterday, just after writing the threnody above, I was driving the car through dense forest lost to mankind two-hundred kilometres northwest of Toronto when the news crackled in from

CBC radio that Helmut Kohl had just presided over a big ceremony in Berlin honouring Stauffenberg and other "conspirators" who had attempted on this date fifty years ago to assassinate Hitler. According to the radio, Kohl called them heroes who had helped to retrieve German honour from the shame of Hitler. Bravo. Bravo. And about time too.

October 25, 1994

Dear Jim,

Your last letter, ostensibly written in July, struck me as something of a *Flaschenpost,** filled with wondrous matter, strange transatlantic musings about a fictitious country named Germany and pipe dreams of "virtual" history, the thing having taken ages (two months, to be precise) to reach these shores and be opened by me, of all people. Oughtn't I to put it softly back into its protective fairy glass bottle and send it off on another voyage, to be picked up someday by someone more innocent and pious who might read it as a puzzling ancient saga?

Where on earth did you light upon the figure of 600,000 Germans (not counting German Jews, Gypsies, and common criminals, I suppose) who resisted Hitler and were imprisoned? Or even thousands upon thousands of Germans actually attempting to rid the world of the Hitler scourge? I'd dearly like to believe you and be able to quote it from a source open to anybody's scrutiny.

And do you really think the Kreisau people or Canaris or Rommel or Beck or any of the men of the "20th July" movement wanted to bring about a disorganization of the German fronts and help the Allied war effort — something that would have had to go under the name of sabotage and betrayal of one's country? As far as there *was* sabotage, it was effected by communists, Jews, slave workers, and prisoners of war; at least that's what I have read and consider likely. The impressively continuous high-level resistance movement from the late thirties onward, especially in the upper echelons of the German army, was at first out simply to prevent war, while still hop-

---

* Bottle-post, message in bottle, to be forwarded by anyone fishing the bottle out of the sea or finding it on the shore.

ing to right the wrongs of Versailles; then, after war had broken out, to reach some honourable armistice and peace, hopefully with some German gains secured. The utmost they were at last willing to go in the direction of betraying their country (as distinct from fighting Nazism and killing Hitler) was that in 1944 in order to put a last-minute stop to Hitler's madness they would take the *risk* of promoting Allied advance and — *horribile dictu* — throw German men, women, and children at the mercy of conquering, marauding armies.

Also, if you suppose the people of the 20th July have not been honoured in Germany, this year's celebration coming as a surprise to you, it simply shows how little anybody not regularly reading German newspapers *can* know about Germany. Apart from neo-Nazis and other stinking things, what facts of German life do, after all, make it into your newspapers and electronic media? Precious little, I dare say. It's a fact that the day of Stauffenberg's bomb at the *Wolfsschanze* (Wolf's Den) has been celebrated annually, at least since the foundation of the Federal Republic, and this year's is special only because it is its fiftieth anniversary.

And President Richard von Weizsäcker the only important government figure to attack the atrocities of the neo-Nazis? That's far off the mark. I haven't seen anybody around *not* attacking them. Which puts paid to your inventing a special cause in Weizsäcker's case. His father, Ernst von Weizsäcker, was not even a clear case of resistance. He was put before the Nuremberg court, and his son Richard as defence counsel could not prevent him from being sentenced to seven years in prison. That was probably unjust, but his role as state secretary in the foreign office under Ribbentrop was anti-Hitler only in the sense that till 1939 he tried to prevent the Führer from doing anything too disastrous, and after that shielded younger men in the foreign office who were indeed part of the resistance.

And yet, and yet, there is some truth in your accusations. It must be your writer's intuition. For these anniversaries, although taken care of by the government and by every paper and TV channel, have been attacked each time from two opposite quarters, which form what one probably has to call an "unholy alliance" (with reference to the "Holy Alliance" against Napoleon, which may not be as much a household word in Canada and America as it is over here). There was always some uneasiness among former German soldiers, not to speak of true-blue conservatives and extreme rightists, about celebrating acts of high treason by the military, however idealistic. I dimly remember that there was stout resistance in the early days of the Bundeswehr (Army of the Federal Republic) against naming barracks after any of the "traitors," and I am sure that Stauffenberg and his friends would, in strictly military terms, have sympathized. On the other side there is the Left, left of the Social Democrats, that is, who on their part are very much opposed to celebrating junkers and bourgeois reactionaries, little better in their eyes than Nazis, even when conspiring to kill Hitler. A whole literature sprang up to prove that many of these resisters had been Hitler fans before, that few were friends of democracy, that some were antisemites, and that in fact they had no intention of turning Germany into a colony of the West, let alone making it anti-fascist in the communist sense. Ought the Stauffenbergs, etc., be celebrated at the expense of the true and principled communist and socialist fighters and martyrs, they asked. Moreover, almost all the good Germans trying to educate themselves and the other post-war Germans into a people repenting of their Nazi past were against the highlighting of German resistance. They saw that as an attempt at national self-acquittal, allowing "the" Germans to hide behind the valour and sacrifice of the few. Thus German celebrations of your German resistance heroes have indeed always been disputed and in a way flawed. But how could it have been otherwise? And of course just as the communists and other Left groupings doubted the legitimacy of the 20th July people as models for a better Germany, the non- and anti-communists saw, and still see, no reason to honour the communist anti-fascist resistance, especially if that resistance consisted of pulling strings from the safe haven of Moscow, as in the case of Pieck and Ulbricht.[21] And if one believes in liberal parliamentary democracy, there is some logic in that.

For, after all, the communists were bent on destroying the Weimar democracy as much as the Nazis. And if you allow me to have my own little stab at "virtual" history: if in 1933 the communists had made it in Germany instead of the Nazis, who can say what horrors they might have committed, guided by Moscow? And would we then, after their defeat and downfall, have been happy with honouring Nazi resistance and Nazi martyrdom, which there surely would have been plenty of?

---

21 Wilhelm Pieck, President of communist Germany 1949-1960. — Walter Ulbricht, factual Head of State of communist Germany 1960-1971.

But that's probably exactly what you think yourself, as you are no friend of the communists and even tell me that they are worse than the Nazis. That is saying a lot, though. In the face of what they both did and what more they both would have been perfectly capable of doing, there is perhaps not much point in marking out differences. And of course you are right that since the end of the last war, the Nazi threat has been largely imaginary, compared with the communist threat and communist reality. And yet we must give it to them that their ideas and ideals were universal, humanist, as they loved to call them, excluding in principle no one willing to embrace them, while Hitler's utopia was inexorably built on the corpses and the slavery of those not endowed with the Chosen Genes.

It is for another reason that I find you a bit strict on the communist "Ossis" with their recent nostalgia for the old GDR, though I must confess I too feel some revulsion. I think it safe to definitely rule out a return to communism in the Five Laenders.[22] Not even the PDS[23] is really communist. What the Ossis resent and what fires their nostalgia right now is that on the fall of the communist regime they woke up finding themselves not only in a minority position — that was inevitable — but in a position of abysmal inferiority, something irreconcilable with their, or anybody's, self-esteem. In that light some return to things of the past — something at least theirs — is only too understandable. Under such circumstances — not altogether different from what the Germans as a whole had to grapple with after the fall of Nazism — to become extremely critical of the victors of history, to point to their hilarious lack of insight, to resent their real or imagined triumphalism, reject their humiliating superiority, even their generosity and compassion, is only "Normal-Null". With the good will of the Old Laenders guaranteed, I think it will pass. And can you really imagine Germany threatening the world with communist rule? Or, for that matter, Germany — any Germany — "trying to lord it over the world again"? I boldly venture to say that for today's Germans, that is pure foreigners' fantasy, even a perverse sort of flattery.

"The German is either at your throat or at your feet"? Well, I'm particularly hardened against shockers of this kind, even if aimed at

---

22 *Five Laenders.* The former communist Germany, east of the Elbe, joining the Federal Republic in 1990.

23 *PDS. Partei des Demokratischen Sozialismus* (the 1990 re-named *SED, Sozialistische Einheitspartei Deutschlands,* of the former GDR).

me personally. (And why, if it's "the" German, should I be an exception?) Horrible or not, the question is whether or to what extent it's true. Is it really an old saying? And if it is, exactly how old? I know that Churchill said it, but I wonder what empirical fact it was originally meant to refer to. Did it mean individual Germans as immigrants in British countries or colonies with an image of underdog trying to survive or prosper one way or another? (As price-cutting competitors for jobs and markets, they were really not much liked.) Interestingly there seems to be a West-East cliché here, for a similar notion occurs in Germany toward the Russians or the Slavs, sometimes even including Germans of some of the former border provinces. At bottom, the saying seems to come straight from any establishment's mouth, from the *beati possidentes*, the masters, the master race, expostulating about "impossible" serfs, slaves, upstarts, latecomers, dangerous and comtemptible at the same time, who will never be mentally balanced, never gentlemen. Churchill (and you) are of course thinking of the German nation or state. But apart from the First and Second World Wars ("at your throat") and 1945 and afterwards ("at your feet"), I'm unable to see what general historic experience it could reflect. I read that you bet your bottom dollar that I didn't know of extermination camps. Which I dare say would be a safe bet for a large majority of Germans under Hitler, no matter how often this has, for threadbare reasons, been doubted. But let me be precise, for the record.

One evening in January or February 1945 a roommate of mine at the barracks at Detmold, where we were training for officers of the reserve, a dark-haired boy from Bonn, known among us for his anti-Nazi views, told us that the Jews in Poland were being murdered in boxcars by gas. We said we did not believe him (actually the detail of the boxcar was wrong; it was trucks, as we know today), and the subject was dropped.

Secretly I thought it monstrous of him to peddle such obvious horror myths fabricated most likely by the same old British bureau that had invented the hacked-off children's hands of 1914 Belgium. You see that even being told the truth was not equivalent to knowing — unless you counted the inveterate Nazi-haters who would believe anything of them, even that which accidentally they had failed to commit, such as turning Jewish corpses into soap, breeding racially valuable babies in institutions, putting fire to the Reichstag, killing fifteen thousand Polish officers at Katyn, or gassing hopelessly wounded German soldiers (as Thomas Mann informed his German listeners in one of his wartime radio messages).

The other day I decided to trace the whereabouts of that committed anti-Nazi boy and ask him how he had come by the knowledge he had tried to pass on to us despite the fact that two of our group were absolute Hitler fanatics. (Decent chaps, though; they didn't inform on him.) When at last I discovered him in his retreat at Rheinbach, I expected to be told of a Catholic resistance cell with access to secret information or something of the kind. But his tale was disappointingly simple, and strange at the same time. On home leave around Christmas 1944, he had eavesdropped on his father and an SS officer. Both men were moved to tears as the SS man told his boyhood friend in no uncertain terms about the horrors Germans were committing against the Jews in the East.

Had my friend told us that in 1945, I might just have considered believing him.

But then, would it have made much difference? In practical terms? Would I have joined him when a little later he reported to our top sergeant that he could no longer undertake to train for officer, as he was "not in agreement with the regime"? I wish I could believe that I would have. (The sergeant asked him if he thought that *he* was in agreement with the regime — but would it do anybody any good if young lives like his were sacrificed at the front instead? The boy insisted, but a few days later it didn't matter one way or the other, as training came to an abrupt end and the lot of us were rushed into the Ruhr pocket before the Americans closed it.)

Well, that boy, in contrast to me, was at least aspiring to be numbered one day among your 600,000!

A fortnight ago I watched your *schreckliches Mädchen* on TV, which had completely bypassed me at the time of its cinema release. Yes, it's an impressive film, which is the more an achievement as, on the other hand, it's all teaching and propaganda. A pity I used up all the ammunition to fire at it when talking in my last letter about "beady-eyed teenage researchers."

Yes, I'm becoming more and more critical of the *schrecklich* good (and young) people feeling so damn superior to the old and guilty for not wanting their past dragged into the light of an uncomprehending present. Which is not the same as liking these diehards or holding them up as models. If asked, I would always advise them to come out on their own accord and make a clean breast of it.

On rereading your letter, I stopped at your sentences about 100 per cent war guilt on one side (Germany), implying 100 per cent innocence on the other. Of course you're being ironic here. But I wonder how deep your irony runs.

On the face of it, everybody assumes that innocence is good, while guilt is bad for you. But if a disaster of the size of the Second World War occurs, to maintain that everyone on the scene except Germany was innocent makes mighty nations like Britain, France, America, or Russia look kind of silly. How could they remain innocent? Were they living in a different world?

On closer scrutiny, innocence loses its attractiveness, being appropriate for children and imbeciles: not fit company for a self-respecting nation. That's what I told my countrymen in my first political book, when I saw them struggling all they could to deny Germany's guilt. Thus they felt hugely tickled by A. J. P. Taylor's endeavours to place responsibility for the Second World War squarely with the Allies, in particular the British. They mistook for sympathy with Germany what I considered Taylor's patriotism. I maintained that Taylor was simply sick of seeing his countrymen still on their bellies before Hitler as an omnipotent god or demon. When a nation involved in such a war does in fact succeed in warding off guilt, the only innocence that can emerge is that of non-accountability.

In A. J. P. Taylor's terms, Germany was something of an "innocent" avalanche that the other nations had not had the sense to take precautions against. Was that to be taken as a compliment by Germans? I for one preferred the status of someone held capable of guilt.

Well, Jim, you tell me that you can't help feeling so sad and so mixed about what you write to me, even regretting that we ever started this correspondence. I do hope that will pass. I feel different. Most of the time I'm happy to be able to talk about my life and my country to someone fairly representative of the West and ready to listen. But your feeling of despair about our venture is perhaps a sign to think of bringing it to an end before we tire of it or start moving in circles.

Anyway, I wish you every success with your new book, *Crimes and Mercies*. The chapter you sent me is very forceful and well reasoned. Please don't mar it by exaggerating details of the treatment of German PoWs by the French and Americans. It was quite bad enough as it is. No doubt there was a policy of senselessly stripping us of our

belongings, of things that might have kept many of us from freezing
and dying in the camps. But not a few, including me, kept their pay
books and diaries. Almost all watches, it is true, were pinched by the
guards, but many prisoners held on to valuables, especially rings,
which some of them later traded for food or cigarettes. I should
hate to have this pointed out by people who would like to deny the
whole thrust of your comparison between the Russians and the West.

Meanwhile there has been a long and good review about *my* book
in *Die Zeit.* I could hardly believe it after these eight months of near
silence in the quality papers.

R.

March 17, 1995

Dear Richard,

Your last letter struck me at the waterline. Reading your criticism of my
Flaschenpost, *which I perhaps should put back in the water to continue
its lonely (and futile?) wanderings — what a wonderful image. I thought,
I'm not up to this. My ignorance is appalling. How dare I venture into
debate with this so well informed man, even if to demonstrate each other's
ignorance is part of our purpose.*

Enlightenment is painful for the one being enlightened.

*So I confess to the minor charge right away, to avoid more torture. I
did not know how much the Germans had done to honour and spread the
fame of the resistance leaders. Thank you. But still I cavil: is there indeed
a Stauffenberg Allee in Berlin of equal size, length, width, and overall
importance as the Clay Allee?*

*Whatever the answer, and however embarrassing to me my ignorance is
when exposed, I am glad to know about this.*

*But I plead innocent to the graver charge that must follow if I do not
satisfy your question beginning, "Where on earth did you light upon the
figure of 600,000 Germans ... to have resisted Hitler and been caught
and imprisoned?" You would "dearly like to believe" me, you say, and to
quote from a source open to anyone's scrutiny, but not from a Flaschenpost!
I am very happy to say that I got that information from a very pertina-
cious researcher, a man who finds and stores nuts of knowledge the way
our red squirrels tuck the walnuts into the ground around here in Octo-*

ber. He is Peter Hoffmann, the Kingsford Professor of History at McGill University and author of several books and articles on the German resistance, published by, among others, Harvard University Press and the MIT Press. In his book The History of the German Resistance 1933-45, *he says that more than three million Germans were held in jail or prison for political reasons between 1933 and 1945. Of these, some 800,000 were imprisoned for active resistance to the Nazis. Many others had fled the country. These Germans were the only significant internal resistance movement in the whole world during the war. Many Soviet citizens resisted the Stalinists, but not at the highest levels, and not until they had been liberated by the Germans. Only in Germany were there any attempts on the life of the leader, only in Germany did high officers secretly deliver important intelligence to the enemy during wartime, only in Germany did senior officers such as admirals and generals risk their lives and their families, to bring down the regime. The second in command of the Nazi party, Rudolf Hess, defected to the British in an attempt to bring the war to an end in 1941. The British made no attempt to use him to bring down Hitler. They judged him mad and imprisoned him for the rest of his life. The most famous general of the war, Erwin Rommel, was ordered by Hitler to choose between execution and suicide for his part in the resistance. The head of German military intelligence, Admiral Wilhelm Canaris, "took breathtaking risks to advance the cause of resistance to Hitler" by passing top-secret information to the Allies. He was hanged in the concentration camp Flossenbrück in April 1945.*

Churchmen such as Pastor Niemöller, Bishop von Galen, aristocrats, leaders and officers such as Fabian von Schlabrendorf, were pushed aside, or ignored or treated with contumely by the victorious Allies.[24] The widow of one officer, Col. Georg Hansen, who had been executed by Hitler for resistance, lived in grief and poverty after the war because she was refused a pension, and her husband's bank account was for a long time blocked by the Allies. After strong British pleas to President Truman, the prisoner Ernst von Weizsäcker was finally released, when his sentence was reduced to time already served. He died less than a year later, on August 4, 1951. As the English author Patricia Meehan has shrewdly concluded, "It was

---

24 Martin Niemöller (see Note 11). Clemens August Graf von Galen, Bishop of Münster, preached against the Nazi doctrine of race and against the killing of the mentally handicapped during the war. Because of his popularity Hitler saved him for treatment after the war. Fabian von Schlabren-dorff was one of the men of the 20th of July. He was condemned to death, but the end of the war intervened.

*not the imprisonment for years of an innocent man which the [British]
Foreign Office deprecated, so much as the incompetence of the American
judges. The Von Weizsäcker Trial File listed in the Foreign Office index is
not, alas, to be found. No doubt it still exists somewhere in the weeders'
limbo. "[25]*

*After the attempt on Hitler's life in July 1944, which ended in mass
executions of resistance leaders by the Gestapo, all Churchill could think
to tell the House was that "the highest personalities in the German Reich
are murdering one another, or trying to, while the avenging Armies of the
Allies close upon the doomed and ever-narrowing circle of their power. "[26]*

*Sir John W. Wheeler-Bennett, a senior Foreign Office adviser, thought
that "It is to our advantage therefore that the [Hitler] purge should
continue, since the killing of Germans by Germans will save us from
future embarrassments of many kinds. "[27] In your letter you speak of many
Germans' reluctance after the war to celebrate acts of high treason.
Stauffenberg, in strictly military terms, you say, "would have sympathized" with certain post-war measures taken by the Bundeswehr to avoid
honouring "traitors." It seems to me that here it is you, Richard, saying
that although on the one hand Hitler's regime was criminal, on the other
hand it was the only legitimate one. Ye gods. Talk about* Flaschenpost.
*Where is your logic? You cannot have it that Hitler was a legitimate
criminal, while Stauffenberg was only criminal. Then you go on with
definitions of the various motives for resistance, showing clearly how the
resistance people are now being used by many Germans as "an attempt at
national self-acquittal...so the celebrations have always been flawed. But
how could it have been otherwise?" This describes on a small scale the
confusion that I am trying to show befuddles Germans on much more
important matters today.*

*There are many people in the West who during the war and to this day
say the resistance leaders were only trying to mitigate the danger for
Germany. What is wrong with that? They further say this began to
happen only when Hitler started to lose, which is untrue. There was at
least one attempt on him before Stalingrad [in 1943], and many plots
before then to stop him somehow. For the majority of the people inside
Germany and for everyone outside, Germany without Hitler was prefer-*

25 Patricia Meehan, *The Unnecessary War,* London, Sinclair-Stevenson, 1992, p
   376.
26 Hansard, Series 5, Vol. 402, 2 August 1944, col 1487.
27 Foreign Office Papers 371/39062, C 9896.

able to Germany with him. And that is what all these people proposed, even those who can easily be presumed to have been as cynical as the Allied leaders thought.

In essence, all the Allied leaders during the war — except Stalin, on occasion — were saying that all Germans are either Hitler or Hitler's. Under no condition could they be distinguished one from the other, or judged apart from each other. That was why the surrender had to be unconditional.

Let us examine the logic of this idea of unconditional surrender. It must begin with unconditionally condemning all Germans as "Hitler's," or else there would be some Germans virtuous enough to negotiate a conditional surrender. But since Hitler was already headed for the gallows at Nuremberg, to condemn them all as "Hitler's" was to say, in effect, kill them all. Exactly here a condition had to enter the idea of no conditions, or else the Allies would have been guilty of a far worse crime than any Hitler committed. Here is the great divide in Allied policy, as some people actually began to implement the logic of the unconditional surrender, and others fought it tooth and nail, in the occupying forces, in the U.S. Senate, in the cabinets of Canada and the U.K., in the press, in the Churches.

The Morgenthau-Eisenhower Plan, which was approved by Roosevelt and Churchill in Canada in 1944, proposed an open-ended devastation of Germany. In its unconditioned state, the plan proposed that the Germans would be reduced to serfs, hand-working a prostrate farm state, the land where Germany used to be. The Allies began to implement this plan in 1944, against prisoners. The sacrifices to be exacted were scaled down to the appalling twenty million to die, the number Clemenceau said [at the time of the First World War] was the surplus of Germans in the world, and also the number envisaged to die under the Morgenthau-Eisenhower Plan. Even that proved too much for the Allies to stomach, so the vengeance was reduced to the imposition of widespread starvation without any specific announced death goal. But the Allies knew that the deaths beyond the normal rate would amount to millions, because Ambassador Robert Murphy said so, in his report of March 1947 to the United States State Department.[28]

The Morgenthau-Eisenhower Plan was a crime of monstrous magnitude. That it was eventually arrested in western Germany, but after many

---

28 Murphy Papers, Hoover Institute on War, Peace and Revolution, Stanford, California. See *Crimes And Mercies* (Note 22) for further interpretation.

millions of deaths, was due to leaders who were compassionate, intelligent, wise, fundamentally Christian and firmly democratic. Two of the most magnanimous men of this period, U.S. President Herbert Hoover and Prime Minister Mackenzie King of Canada, were practicing churchgoers who were quite ready to feed the enemy at cost to themselves and to their country. After the war, King said that what the world needed was Peace, Work and Health, not revenge, while Hoover told the American military governor, Lucius Clay, that "feeding the enemy requires no debate with me since it must be done for many reasons."[29]

If in the German mind today there is, as you imply, an uneasy equating of Hitler with legitimacy, of Stauffenberg with treachery, of resistance with cheating, it is for exactly the same reason that I have described before to you, when I criticized you Germans' inability to protest against Allied outrages against Germans, and many others, including Italians, Austrians, Hungarians, and so on. And that reason is Germany's moral confusion.

I also take issue with your statement that "we must give it to them [the communists] that their ideas were universal, humanist ... excluding in principle no one willing to embrace them." I was amazed to read this. I would have thought that there was no one left alive who believed this, unless maybe a few creaky old former Komsomolskis in a muddy village along the Yenisei. Whether you speak of Marx, Lenin, or Stalin, it is all one: their so-called ideas were rigidly exclusionary, viciously selfish, and aimed at dictatorship, not just of the proletariat, as Marx said, or of the party, as Lenin had it, but a dictatorship of one man, as Stalin did it. I am not talking about some supposed Stalinist perversion of supposedly good Leninist or Marxist ideals, but about the insane hatreds of Lenin that were carried into practice in Russia against scores of millions of people. For the full almost unbelievable horror of Lenin's ideas and practices as they were before, during, and after the revolution, you can't do better than read Dmitri Volkogonov's new biography, Lenin. *It is clear that even before the revolution, the Leninist-Bolsheviks abhorred the very ideas that you said the communists espoused. They drove the exponents of such ideas out of the party, out of the legislature, out of the country — the Mensheviki, and others. And they tried to drive out of the country, or into internal exile, or else they murdered, everyone who opposed their crazed Leninism, which so far as I can see, aimed only at arrogating total control of the whole country to a few greedy madmen in Moscow.*

---

29 Herbert Hoover, An American Epic, Chicago, Regnery, 1959, 64, Vol. IV, pp 162-3.

No doubt there were in the German resistance some few who believed in the noble ideals you mentioned, but let us not traduce them with the epithet communist. Or flatter Stalin with their idealism.

I cannot agree with you about A. J. P. Taylor, the British historian who described the causes of the Second World War. I have no idea why you say that Taylor was sick of seeing his countrymen still on their bellies before Hitler as an omnipotent god or demon. I do not believe for a minute that Taylor thought the Germans were an avalanche, "innocent" or not. My understanding of Taylor is that he was the most honest of all the Allied historians, and had no reverence at all for the received opinions. He said "boak" to those received opinions, because he had found the evidence after lots of digging. And the evidence was that the war aim in the First World War was to find out "who's to be master." And as everyone knows, it was the botched settlement of the question, the Allied betrayals of their promises and so on, that led directly to the ruin of Germany and the rise of Hitler. And then, as Taylor said, "The documents at the Nuremberg trials were chosen not only to demonstrate the war-guilt of the men on trial but to conceal that of the prosecuting Powers."[30] I saw not much sympathy for any nation in his work, but only truth shining through a generalized sympathy for poor, mistaken, shaken humankind.

And I guess that is a good place to end this Flaschenpost.

J.

April 17, 1995

Dear Jim,

For a man-of-war, struck at the waterline, you muster a lot of firepower. At least you hit on a very weak spot in my letter when you attacked my account of A. J. P. Taylor. I think I had better agree with everything you say about him right away (except that he didn't say "boak" but "goak" when confronted with sanctified phoniness). To my detriment, I hadn't reread him for more than thirty years and relied overmuch on what I had then written about him rather high-handedly. Looking into his book now, I realize how right you

---

30 A. J. P. Taylor, *The Origins of the Second World War*, Penguin 1965, p. 36.

are, but also how many of his general tenets fall in with deep-rooted beliefs of mine. ("The historian should seek to anticipate the judgments of the future rather than repeat those of the past. ... about the folly of reparations ... The unique quality in Hitler was the gift of translating commonplace thoughts into action. He took seriously what was to others mere talk. ... If Western morality seemed superior, this was largely because it was the morality of the status quo, Hitler's was the immorality of revision.")[31] I am in fact unable to say whether Taylor and I happened to think alike or whether I drew this wisdom from him and then forgot about the source.

Having conceded that much, let me try to explain to you and, head bowed, to myself, how I came to write about him the way I did — in 1963, that is. The context was not a historical book but a series of more than a hundred short, pointed politico-literary dialogues between a father and his son. As I said in my last letter, in 1963 I was warning my countrymen about the double-edgedness of the innocence they were affecting in the face of Allied accusations, a message that originally had nothing to do with Taylor. But as Taylor's book came out just then and seemed so much of a godsend to my fellow Germans, proving them innocent ("Non Anglus sed Angelus," as Pope Gregory had it) I — in my then still-youthful poetical fervour — made so bold as to "reveal" far more of him than his text warranted, as you have made me realize. I obviously made improper use of what I thought must have been the hidden motives firing him while he delved into the London archives. I imputed to him an undeclared wish to de-demonize Hitler and Germany and, by the same token, give his own country back some of the dignity of a free agent as against a mere victim of German evil. In fact, there is one fundamental element in his book that points that way and may excuse me somewhat, and that is his a priori decision as a historian to refrain from moral judgment ("talk of guilt") where the agents are sovereign states. If the First World War was indeed about "Who is to be master?," to blame and despise Germany for entering the fray a second time made almost as little sense as blaming an avalanche for following the laws of physics.

As I look again at your letter, it strikes me that perhaps both of us read into Taylor something of ourselves, and that your reading is the better because you happen to be more like him than I am.

31 A. J. P. Taylor, ibid., p. 31, p. 73 et pass., p. 99, p. 100. (218)

But back to Stauffenberg.

I think the Clay Allee owes its existence and prominence to the time of the Russian blockade and reflects the relief and the gratitude for the deliverance of the city from that stranglehold. But there is also a Stauffenberg Strasse, not an Allee, to be sure, and shorter, but it touches on the Bendler Block, where he was shot and has the advantage of being more centrally placed than the Clay Allee, which is in Dahlem.

You take me to task for pondering the treason question of the 20th July. And of course my words, like so many others of mine in our correspondence, owe something to the fool's privilege I trust I'm enjoying while writing letters in a language not my own to you, a non-German bent on putting me straight.

In this spirit, let me ask you to allow for at least the *possibility* of unstraightforward issues in history. I mean, before putting it all down to German moral befuddlement, let's look at the facts and implications without foreknowledge of whether and where the moral axe may or may not eventually fall.

To my bafflement, you say that "for the majority of the people inside Germany...Germany without Hitler was preferable to Germany with him." If you believe that, and especially if you take that as an account of what the Germans actually thought in, say, 1936, you may of course draw all kinds of fantastic inferences. But as far as I remember, even for those who were more or less anti-Nazi (and there were indeed not a few hating the Party, the SA, the SS, Rosenberg, Streicher, despising Goebbels and Dr. Ley, making fun of Goering, and so on),[32] — Hitler himself, the Führer and head of state, chief of a proud new army, had risen above the reach of criticism. It seems that most Germans, for whom only four years before he had been but one of those shady gesticulating extremists, now simply couldn't allow themselves to face anything negative about him. Rejecting the person of Hitler, after so much had changed and was changing around them, would have left these Germans in a void they dared not contemplate.

---

32 Julius Streicher. Editor of the anti-Semite weekly *Der Stürmer*. — Dr. Robert Ley, notorious drunkard, leader of the *Arbeitsfront* ("Labor Front" = Nazi Trade Union).

Among those changes were the undoubted blessings Hitler had brought them, which they were sure no one but he would have been capable of: from full employment and an end to reparations to the return of the Saar, the reunification with Austria and the Sudetenland, the *Autobahnen,* the new respect the common worker and peasant was enjoying, and then the quick overthrow of the French and British armies that had threatened Germany from the west in a war most Germans believed had been forced on Germany. Even those at the top of German society who could think of alternatives to Nazism were loath to propose a return to Weimar and its latter-day nightmares. The question what or whom to put in Hitler's place was the one question even the conspirators were openly or secretly afraid of having to answer. *They* knew that Hitler was responsible for everything that was now wrong with Germany, but in a country without public debate and a lot of propaganda instead, the mass of the people had little idea of those wrongs after Hitler had drawn the teeth of the SA in 1934,[33] and certainly didn't like to attribute the wrongs they did see to Hitler himself: that would have been too painful. Even the workers who had voted for the Social Democrats (SPD) or the Communists (KPD) in the time of Weimar were now content to be in agreement with most of what Hitler seemed to stand for. The secret opposition in fact despaired of the task of explaining the need for Hitler's death in the crash course of revelations necessary after it had been effected.

The problem was that Germany, the Fatherland, still meant a lot to people in those days, and that was what Hitler (not his party) together with the Wehrmacht had come to represent. Strange as it may seem now, Hitler was considered the least Nazi (i.e., despicable) of the brown-shirted bunch. By a secret process, easy to explain in psychological or sociological terms, he had become Germany. Loving Germany, the German people needed a human being to represent the object of their love, and even if Hitler hadn't consciously cast himself in that image, there would have been nobody,

---

33 In the night of the "long knives", June 30th 1934, Hitler ordered the SS to murder the chief of the SA, his long-term comrade Röhm, and the other high SA leaders under suspicion of rebelling against him. This, although a brutal act of arbitrary "justice" by the Chief of State, raised Hitler's reputation with the German middle classes, who had feared the rule of the proletarian SA.

after Hindenburg's death, to challenge him in the role. It's horrible what people see or refuse to see when there is an overwhelming need for it. It's what falling in love is mostly about. Think of Little Red Riding Hood. How could she mistake the wolf for her beloved grandmother, seeing as she did the paws, the ears and the mouth. She loved her so much and wanted to be reunited with her so dearly that instead of running away and calling for help, she went nearer and nearer, fascinated by the strangeness of it all. What of course contributed to the disaster was that the child had forgotten Granny for a while, had neglected her duties, as the Germans thought they had done in the Roaring Twenties of the Weimar Republic. Back at last on the right path and eager to make good, the child was in no mood to be thwarted in her drive toward grandmother. There was the house, the well-known clothes, the bed. Just as Hitler, from the "Day of Potsdam"[34] onward, seemed to represent the older and better Germany of Hindenburg and the kaiser. Even most German Jews would have liked to have been Hitler's after he had become Granny — if only he had let them.

Now vis-à-vis that, imagine the plight of a German opposition. They also loved the fatherland and wanted every German to love it and continue loving it after they had done away with Hitler. They would probably not have gone to war for the righting of Versailles, but of course knew the equivalent of Polonius's advice to Laertes that if you can't avoid a fight, you should teach the other fellow a lesson not to be forgotten.

The dilemma they never quite knew how to solve was how to kill the wolf without killing Little Red Riding Hood and Grandma, with whom he had become one. For as you point out correctly, the Allies, wanting to determine who's to be master, and therefore not really interested in distinguishing between Hitler and the Germans, were quite prepared to kill the wolf together with what he had swallowed. And that didn't exactly make things easier for the conspirators. As soon as a war was on, killing the head of state came uncomfortably close to giving the fatherland, fighting against enemies determined on its destruction, a stab in the back.

---

34 On the 21st March 1933, at the opening of the first Nazi Parliament, Hitler staged a public handshake with the senile German President, Field Marshall Paul von Hindenburg, above the grave of Frederick the Great in Potsdam.

They were German and philosophical enough to understand that in order to save a trace of Germany's honour, they had no choice but to act outside the law — in fact, risk dishonour in the eyes of the German people and perhaps even before the eventual judgment of history. Breaking their military oath of loyalty and attempting to deliver their country of the evil of Hitler, they would inevitably work into the hands of the enemies and not only deprive their country of any chance of "being master," but place her at the mercy of a Stalin and his crony Roosevelt.

Now, deciding to do that is a very lonely and desperate thing. They planned it time and again; time and again circumstances interfered, but at last they did do it, and just because it was anything but a straightforward issue, I admire them wholeheartedly and want to see them honoured.

But like some saints of the Church, they can hardly be put up as models for ordinary Christians in ordinary times. Extreme doings have their place and honour in extreme situations. Lonely decisions of the Stauffenberg kind are beyond the scope of rules and laws. They are merely trivialized if turned into household truths. I might perhaps have voted for a Stauffenberg Kaserne (i.e., Barracks), for after all he was not only the failed assassin of Hitler but had some military merits as well. But I would understand the opposition of professional soldiers, feeling responsible for what an army is meant to be. Recruits have to learn a lot of unpleasant things, and for those of a free and democratic country, the hardest is perhaps to obey or face consequences. If that isn't accepted, the very idea of an army is being rejected. One can do that, but then one should be honest and declare oneself a pacifist, which Stauffenberg certainly wasn't.

I like your, i.e., Peter Hoffmann's, summary of the German resistance movement, hoping that it is reliable. My own *Lexikon* of the German resistance[35] has it that there were about seven thousand German resistance fighters known by name. So there must be some difference in definitions between my *Lexikon* and Hoffmann's book to explain the vast difference between 7,000 and 800,000. I never credited the German opposition the way I should obviously have done, and I'll try to get hold of Hoffmann's book. But of course it's not an accident that these things are largely unknown, have been

35 Wolfgang Benz and Walter H. Pehle, *Lexikon des deutschen Widerstandes.* Frankfurt am Main 1994.

ignored, denied, or played down. Anything that told in favour of the Germans or put the Allies and the Nazi victims in a not so favourable light is still not PC in Germany. In fact, this year of so much remembering is widely used to put a new lease on life into this kind of cooking the books — and all allegedly for the best of Germany and the world.

That's very much your situation. But the guns are now also pointed at me, because in my latest book, and in the speeches I have been making since, I sort of closed ranks with you and took issue with the pat way Russian, Polish, Czechoslovak, American, British, and French war and post-war crimes are being swept off the board by simply declaring them natural effects of (German) immoral causes. Nobody except the hardened sinners of the Right seems to notice how flawed this time-honoured argument is.

All misdeeds have causes, even Hitler's. And we can of course talk about them as extenuating circumstances, when Russians, Poles, and Czechs drive Germans from their native homes, plunder, torture, murder, or rape them in the tens of thousands — or when Americans keep German PoWs by the millions after the war in camps without shelter and at starvation levels, or — though this is different (because part of the actual war) — when the British air force terrorizes the civilian inhabitants of German cities, with Dresden standing out as a particularly nasty piece of senseless destruction. But the issue is innocence; and causes, however extenuating, cannot constitute innocence. It is said that these Allied crimes were not crimes by Poles or Americans or British, but crimes the Germans — via Hitler — committed against themselves. The Poles, Brits, Americans, etc., they say, were mere links in the chain reaction Hitler and the Germans set in motion. But that's the way most criminals defend themselves, saying they had no choice. The Allies, the Czechs, and the Poles allegedly had no choice but to answer Hitler's crimes by crimes of their own, which thereby lost the quality of crimes and became effects (of causes). Just as if these people, at their desks or with their Kalashnikovs, had been automatons, not free moral agents, not even after Hitler and Germany had been put down. As if Poland had been *forced* to grab German territory, even Stettin to the "wrong" side of the Oder! Or that Bomber Harris[36] had had no mind of his

---

36 "Bomber Harris". Sir Arthur Travers Harris, commander-in-chief, Bomber Command, RAF, 1942-45.

own and had not *decided* to wipe out German cities, but simply couldn't help doing it in revenge for Coventry. Isn't that ridiculous? As if the war against millions of German civilians, which was in fact meant to end the war (and incidentally cost also the lives of some fifty thousand Allied airmen), would not have taken place if only Hitler had abstained from bombing Coventry!

In what light do people trotting out this sort of argument put the Allies? Were they zombies who could only react to Hitler in kind? It's the irony of innocence once again. Taken seriously, it lands us with the absurdity that only the Bad are subject to moral obligations, while the Good merely function in chains of cause and effect. I think, fifty years after the war, that this is particularly unfair to Germany, the only country in history willing to accept her guilt and atone for it.

Well, the communists. My article in the *Freibeuter* about the two German defeats/liberations, the one in 1945 and the other in 1989, with all kinds of similarities in the reactions of the defeated/liberated in either case, has just come out. As so often on reading in cold blood something of mine printed, I find it too dense, dehydrated, as it were, not amenable enough to the way people read texts nowadays.

Somebody told me that he read my book *Normal-Null* with reward three times over. Moving to hear, isn't it? But also damning. Anyway, I've done all in my power to say in my article what I felt no one else would say. I began with a longish quotation from the diary of Rudolf Hoess, the sometime commandant of Auschwitz, (written in a Polish prison cell in 1947), without revealing the identity of the writer and replacing the Nazi terms by communist equivalents. Amazing how exactly his beliefs and concessions square with what we have been hearing from former communists after 1989. Still, I can't follow you in your absolute denunciation of them. Now that the war against them seems over, I mourn with the victims of their world experiment, but can't see a point any longer in denying the nobility and fascination of their vision. I don't know and don't care much about Lenin, but I always like to take movements and ideas at their best when comparing, and then communism wins against Nazism hands down.

R.

May 8, 1995

Dear Richard,

I have finished my new letter to you on May 8, 1995. When I began this book with you, even when I began this letter, I did not realize we would be writing to each other on the fiftieth anniversary of the end of the war. Now I feel we are called on to say something special to each other today. The wild celebrations of fifty years ago in the Western democracies, repeated far and wide today, have for a moment wiped clear my memory of the time between, so when I look back at May 8, 1945, there is a grey plain between me and a distant land where great events are happening that I can no longer remember exactly, except the joy of the bells in Toronto on a morning such as this one today, bright, warm, happy, and the thought that at last now my father and my brothers and my sister will all come home, and the dog will bark with excitement and we will all be happy again. And there you are yourself, young, an enemy in that land far beyond the grey plain, roving around with a machine gun. I cannot congratulate you on your liberation, or expect congratulations from you on our victory. I think of some wise words, of Candide, "Il faut cultiver notre jardin." And of A. J. P. Taylor, "As a private citizen, I think that all this striving after greatness and domination is idiotic; and I would like my country not to take part in it."[37]

I think you Germans have learned a lot, and we have learned only a little. But still, together we have improved the world. It was far better almost everywhere to be alive in 1989 than in 1939. Any six years since 1945 were better for the human race than the war years. No one in his right mind today would volunteer to work for 1939 wages/purchasing power, or have a baby in a hospital run on 1939 principles, or send a child to a 1939 school. More people are alive today on earth than ever before, more are literate, fewer die per capita from disease, war, or famine. In a slow and general way, life for most of us has improved and goes on improving, I believe. So, across fifty years of hatred dying, and fifty years of friendship growing, I salute you. But not your Latin — the quotation from Gregory should read, "Non Angli, sed Angeli"[38]

---

37 A. J. P. Taylor ibid., p. 9 (231)
38 The original in Latin was "Responsum est, quod Angli vocarentur. At ille: 'Bene,' inquit, 'nam et angelicam habent faciem, et tales angelorum in

(Later) A recent survey in a class of bright young law students in a Toronto high school showed that the students had barely heard of the Second World War and Hitler, and that they knew nothing about it. One student hesitantly asked if Winston Churchill was the leader of Britain. No one had heard of Stalin.

All these bright young Canadians looked expectantly at the teacher when one of them asked, "What did Canada have to do with all this?" They didn't know that their country had fought Germany for six years! And these are typical of most young North Americans, who are ignorant of the whole subject.

So while Germans live with the shame and the guilt of it, North Americans know virtually nothing of the war. Of late there has been a strong emphasis on the Holocaust, so that now some people view the war as the background to a pogrom. This reached some kind of nadir in the New Yorker *on May 1, 1995, in an essay trying to account for the "genesis of Hitler's evil." The writer quoted approvingly a filmmaker who believes that "you can't engender the killing, the mass murders, the destruction of six million people..." from Hitler's baby pictures. The stupidity of this would be hilarious if it weren't for the gross misunderstanding of the horrendous subject. Apart from the preposterous notion that one might "engender" killings by interpreting baby pictures, there is the grim concentration on the deaths of six million people, while all the others are overlooked. Some fifty million people died of Hitler's evil, but the filmmaker can see only six million of them. Seen through his lens, the Holocaust, front and centre, masks the tragedy of all the other people in the Second World War. This is the other side of Hitler's deeds: grotesque action produces grotesque reaction, even after fifty years.*

In the late 1980s, as more and more books appeared discussing the Holocaust, which was already the subject of many books, I began to wonder why they were appearing, and what effect they were having. What good did they do? The only possible answer seemed to me, So we can make sure such things never happen again. But all these Holocaust stories had

---

caelis decet esse coheredes.'" This derives from the story of young Englishmen (Angles) being brought before the Pope, who asked what they were called, and "the answer was, 'They are called Angles.' 'It is well,' he said, 'for they have the faces of angels and such should be the co-heirs of the angels in heaven.'" This has been conveyed by the Venerable Bede to Anglo-Saxons as 'Non Angli sed Angeli,' or "Not Angles but angels." All this learned stuff courtesy of the *Oxford Book of Quotations*, London, Oxford University Press, 1953, p. 232.

one fundamental point: Hitler and Germany were evil, the Jews were innocent. So I thought, 'We already know that to everyone except the Nazis, the Jews were no guiltier than anyone else, so the point is Hitler's evil. And what good can come from studying evil?'

I could not see any point, but I did see a danger. Whatever one studies, one tends to imitate. I wanted to read not about vicious people committing crimes, but about those who had overcome evil. I wanted the way out, not the way in. And precisely here I came upon that book titled Avenue of the Righteous *by Peter Hellman, from which I learnt about Raoul Laporterie, whom I have mentioned in an earlier letter. It was while researching his grand and funny story of Jews saved from the Holocaust that I decided I had to give up my ban on Germany and go there to do research. I had already lived in Europe for more than a year, visiting many countries, but I had never gone to Germany. To me, it was the birthplace of famous musicians and a list of bombing targets. So I was apprehensive, almost sick of myself for breaking my forty-year vow, as our train rattled slowly across the rusty old bridge over the Rhine at Strasbourg.*

In Bonn, I met Hans Goertz, who had been a prisoner of war of the French in 1945. Then he was "hired" as a "free worker" by Raoul Laporterie to work in Laporterie's haberdashery in Mont-de-Marsan, near Bordeaux. For hours over white wine in his living room in Bonn, Goertz told me stories of his life after the war with Laporterie, of his kindness, of the odd people who worked for him, of his reconciliation with the French. When he was finished, my assistant turned off the tape recorder, and suddenly Goertz changed. He became more confiding. He leaned forward and quietly said, "When I stood in front of that man, I knew I was saved."

"Saved?"

"From the camp [Buglose]."

"What was the matter with the camp?"

"Twenty-five per cent of the men in that camp died in one month."

My assistant and I tried, but we could get no more out of him, not even the address of the other prisoner who had been at Laporterie's store with him. Goertz clammed up as if he had let go a powerful secret by chance. He had been suppressing this information for more than forty years. And so had the other prisoner, who Goertz told me also refused to discuss it with me. As my assistant and I dug into this amazing story, we needed more detail from Goertz, but he refused to add a word. He would not even reply to my calls or letters. Finally, I sent him several pages of my

*proposed chapter about him, which contained one egregious and deliber-
ate error that I had no intention of publishing. Goertz could not resist
that: he replied, correcting the error and added a few other minor corrections and additions.*

*At first I thought that Goertz had hidden all this because of that well-
known reluctance soldiers have to discuss the horrors they have endured,
à la Heising. But I slowly realized that there was far more to it than that.
Goertz was afraid. And with reason: the establishment people of Germany, France, Canada, the U.K., and the U.S. have turned the whole
subject of Allied post-war treatment of Germany into a minefield. You
have seen the explosions going off around* Other Losses, *but it is far
worse than that.*

*A friend of the farmer Otto Tullius of Bretzenheim was threatened by
police with a bankrupting fine if he continued to dig on Tullius's land
for traces of German prisoners of war in the American camp formerly
there. Count Nikolai Tolstoy in England was bankrupted for exposing
crimes against prisoners of war committed by high members of the British
establishment. One aspect of all this that makes the cover-up necessary in
the minds of the court historians is that they think that to reveal Allied
war crimes makes us complicit in all the war guilt, which reduces German guilt. If we were to be revealed as guilty of the crimes that we did in
fact commit, this absurdist reasoning goes, somehow Hitler's guilt for
Barbarossa or Coventry or Treblinka or Rotterdam would be diminished.
In the same way, it is imagined, to reveal our atrocities against Germany
might "diminish" the Holocaust or German war guilt. What absurdity.
As if anyone could "diminish" these horrors. Does the most insistent of
Holocaust believers say that to study earlier European pogroms against
the Jews diminishes Hitler's crimes? Did the German crimes against the
British diminish British crimes against the Irish? How silly. Yet this is
the reasoning that silences Goertz, and millions of others, for decades,
and still tries to silence Tolstoy, de Zayas, Kimminich, and me. What an
irony for those people that my case and Tolstoy's is proven anew by the
documents revealed with the opening of the archives of the arch silencers
in the KGB.*

*And so it all comes down to this, something it has taken me ten years to
realize: you are in bondage to us, but your bondage is ours. The owner is
enslaved by his ownership of the slave.*

The word slave *is now of course too strong — you are no longer a
slave; your condition changed years ago, into something like an enchant-
ment. You are under a spell, and so are we now, the spell of a wrong*

history. But it is a spell with powerful enforcement. Revisionists are flung in jail for expressing an illegal opinion; whoever denounces allied war crimes is anathematized by the establishment, although massively supported by the surviving victims, post-war immigrants are mercilessly persecuted for alleged minor misdemeanours on their fifty-year-old entry-papers. Throughout the west, Germans as a people are routinely degraded in a manner which would attract prosecution if the victims were blacks or Jews or aboriginal North Americans. All over North America, editors and producers usually refuse to publish stories or letters describing the sufferings of the Germans since 1945.

So my lonely and apprehensive journey across the Rhine into enemy territory at Strasbourg in 1986 has ended with my writing new books about the evil that people do. My only excuse for adding to the record of misery in the world is precisely that — I am adding to it, not repeating something already known. And I am trying to make the point, in Just Raoul *as well as the others, that there were those who acted from conscience and sought to save the victims despite the opposition of the enemy, whether German or Allied. It disgusted me that the ideals for which we had fought had been so cruelly betrayed, and it repelled me that having committed these vast atrocities against Germans, we were nevertheless making innocent young people in Germany carry a weight of shame one can hear in their voices and see in their hanging heads. All this while making them pay enormous sums in reparations.*

In a restaurant in London in 1988, I was being served by a young woman who had a Central European accent, and as I was on my way to Germany to do research, I asked where she came from. She hung her head and said, "Germany."

She really did hang her head. When I commented on this to a young woman in Rheinberg, she told me that she too feels the same way when she is out of Germany. She hates to leave Germany, she said, because she always feels — or is made to feel — so guilty. Then I began to remember hearing stories about how French drivers in France force German cars off the autoroutes at the risk of death.

And then it happened to me, in a village in the south of France. For a year I lived in the village and drove a Volkswagen with German plates. Once when I was walking beside a small highway near the village, a French car deliberately swerved at high speed straight at me, forcing me to jump off the roadside. Someone in the village had decided I was German and was willing to scare me at the risk of death. This is scary stuff. I had no idea who he was, but he must have smirked the next time he saw me in

*the village. Imagine then how much resentment there is among people you
see walking on the street every day in Aachen, their faces masking their
true feelings. What would they do to a Kanadier or Ami or Brit if they
knew they could get away with it? Which is what the Nazis thought. And
what the neo-Nazis think today.*

*Richard, something too like the 1930s is starting. German resentment,
Allied ignorance. Just imagine the dull incomprehension on the faces of
the young law students in Toronto and all over North America and
probably in the U.K. too, when they confront consequences they don't
comprehend of a war they have scarcely heard of. Does it remind you of
something? Such as Versailles, Hitler, And All That Jazz?*

*That's the pessimistic view, I guess, but I started this on a more
optimistic note, so let me remind you of that saying — from Marx? —
that history repeats itself, the first time as tragedy, the second time as
farce. Is that the neo-Nazi movement today? When they stand in front of
the Feldherrnhalle today, is the song they are singing* Deutschland,
Deutschland über Allies? *I think so. In the meantime, dear enemy,*
salut!

J.

July 17, 1995

Dear Jim,

May 8, 1995, though but two months ago, is very much a thing of
the past here. The exhumation and revival of fifty years ago plus a
propaganda war about its *meaning* for today's Germans raged in the
media for so many days a month and hours a day and pages a newspaper that the subject is now dead and virtually untouchable. Which
is a pity. The message I put across in speeches I made at Erkelenz and
Veitshöchheim and that I also tried to spread on TV, is because of
overexposure of the subject now definitely barred from appearing
in print. The speeches made by the big shots, which of course are
being printed, were all of the predictable kind, at best rehashes of
what Weizsäcker in his celebrated speech said ten years ago.

On the more positive side were many individual German voices,
telling, just as you did, their particular story of VE Day: all very
touching, elating, horrible, comical, and altogether impressive for
their variety and incompatibilities.

The contribution I might make under that heading is compara- tively dull. According to my dirt-stained little diary, there were rumours of peace on Sunday, May 6, which was the day I passed out for a couple of minutes before I was at last able to relieve my bowels of the net result of four weeks' PoW rations over the slit trench I just about managed not to slip into. Later there was a religious service. On May 7, farmers and miners were separated from the rest, includ- ing me, and they were marched to another camp (Sinzig) across the Ahr. The weather was at last improving, and the 8th was a picture- book May day. My twenty-four hours' ration was two raw potatoes, two level tablespoons of peas and meat, one of beans, one-half of corned beef, one and one-half of sugar, two of dried milk, one-half of pea meal, one-quarter of lard, one-quarter of apple butter, ten raisins, which my notebook sums up as *erträglich* (tolerable). The only thing still standing out clearly in my living memory is of Allied aircraft thundering in formation up and down the Rhine valley. This we took as confirmation of the rumour about the end of the war.

Faint as my memories of anything else are, I can't detect any rejoicing or satisfaction at the fact. On the contrary, I seem to have mainly resented the pride of the victors up there above us human mud-hogs. Not even the prospect of returning home now that the war was over seems to have made much difference. What kind of home would I return to in a ruined and downtrodden country? What could the future hold for me, at eighteen without proper schooling or trade? Nor was I alone in this pessimism, I think. One certainly allowed oneself secretly a bit more hope of improvement: to be sent to a camp with shelter and beds and cooked meals and perhaps some work to do, and — whyever not? — to be released. But experience advised against hope. And indeed, a couple of days later we were on our way to Bolbec, Normandy, on a three days' train journey with nothing but a sack of potatoes and a big can of drinking water in our freight car and more starvation waiting for us and no idea when we might be allowed to go home.

So much for the end of the war as lived through by PoW Richard Müller.

The meaning of the day for post-war Germany is another matter. In 1962 — schoolmaster, thirty-five, married, two children — I made myself conspicuous by writing a letter to the *FAZ*, suggesting that we celebrate May 8 as our national holiday instead of the uprising of

June 17, 1953, in East Germany against communist misrule. That was something in which, after all, the Federal Republic had not taken part. No other day, I argued, marked so conclusively the end of the Old and Bad, and the beginning of what had meanwhile proved to be the New and Better, something at last to be a little proud of nationally. True, it had been a day of blood and tears and desperation for millions of Germans, but it was a birth, and births are often messy and bloody, even sometimes costing a mother's life. And weren't those Frenchmen whose ancestors were led to the revolutionary guillotine probably just as averse to celebrations of July 14 as the refugees from Silesia and East Prussia would be vis-à-vis my proposal? Thus ran my argument — to little avail, of course. Only some communists applauded.

Now, more than thirty years later, all that has changed. In the run-up to this year's commemoration, Germans were semi-officially supposed to be united in the idea that May 8, 1945, had been a day of liberation, not of defeat or sorrow. Those still opting for the latter alternative were denounced as diehard or neo-Nazi. This public consent, assisted by some brainwashing and propaganda in the media, was broken only late in the day by an advertisement campaign, staged by a splinter group of the liberal FDP *(Freie Demokratische Partei)* and some aged reactionaries from Helmut Kohl's Union,[39] which made the media cartel and the Left the more fierce in their determination to have it all their way. Helmut Kohl tried to quieten the waters by saying what probably most Germans in their new-found broadmindedness accepted: that for the generation with living memories of the day, the answer depended on what had been their particular experiences, and that nobody should try to commandeer anybody's memories. The young in a similar vein said that the Eighth of May ("and all that") really meant nothing to them any longer any way.

Where did that leave me?

What Kohl said and what the young say, I think, is beside the point, the flattening of a serious issue. The question is a political one; it's above the level of whether Kohl individually felt liberated as

---

39 "Kohl's Union". The federation, since Adenauer's time, of the Christian Social Union (only in Bavaria) and the Christian Democratic Union (in the rest of the republic).

a youngster under a blue sky with no more bombs and threats of being drafted to the Volkssturm, or youngsters today choosing not to take an interest in their country and its history. It's to do with facts concerning the Germans as a nation, and insofar as today's Germans are still members of that nation, the question on that level is whether there was liberation or defeat for "Germany" in 1945.

Part one of the answer is clear and straightforward: Germany was liberated from the Nazi regime, whether she liked it or not (and I tend to think that a majority even as early as 1945 liked it). But part two of the answer is irritatingly blurred for many Germans today. They can no longer believe — or face — that Germany was also defeated, humiliated, killed politically, bereft of self-government, occupied, chopped in pieces, deprived of her capital and robbed of a quarter of her geographical body altogether. It was a rare German in 1945 who despaired of himself or his countrymen to the extent of liking that.

Back in 1962 it was still clear to every German that post-war history had not been all fairy tale, in spite of things in the end turning out better than had been feared. This was so much so that my countrymen hated me for emphasizing the obvious good bound up with the sinister.

Now, in 1995, I find that by deleting the national defeat, the humiliation of being at the mercy of the victors, the horrors of the ethnic cleansing, the thefts even beyond the reparations, the mass murder, the mass rape, my countrymen are taking the earnestness out of the acknowledgement of the blessings that May 8 brought. When in 1962 I had asked for it to be made the national holiday, it was in spite of the horrors of defeat. Now, in 1995, on the other hand, I thought it light-brained to rejoice with the French, the Dutch, the Belgians, who had indeed been nothing but freed in 1945. And found myself a second time ranged among the Bad Boys. In 1962, only a German commie was supposed to be able to celebrate May 8. In 1995, only a Nazi was supposed to be able not to.

What is one to learn from this? I'm coming slowly to the conviction that most people are constitutionally unable to accommodate more than one thought in their brain at a time. Any truth not immediately compatible with that single thought is thrown out and projected on to the devil, "until the times do alter." Then they will scratch their heads in wonder how the hell they (or their fathers) could ever have been so blind for so long — and turn to the opposite one-track thought.

Right now the German newspapers are printing more and more articles and letters criticizing the colossal Holocaust monument to be built in Berlin. All kinds of relevant and irrelevant suggestions are being made by Jews and Christians for improving and reducing the size of the thing (a slightly tilted 100 x 100 m concrete plate, 7 m thick with the names of all known Jewish victims on it). But everyone hastens to add that a central monument in Berlin has got to be built. That seems to be the condition for public criticism to be admissible at all. But in order to bring out the real *awe*-fulness of a Holocaust monument in Germany, some kind of fundamental resistance is needed. The ease with which the plans have passed all the necessary stages, the readiness of everyone to fall over their feet in warding off the idea of not being in favour of it, is in truth destroying its foundations even before they have been laid. It is supposed to be, and is in fact dubbed, a *Mahnmal*, which my German-English dictionary, in want of a better equivalent, renders as "memorial" (*Denkmal*). Now this edifice, if built, will most certainly be a memorial, namely, in memory of the Jews, murdered at the behest of a German government, and it will, one hopes, also be a *Mahnmal* serving as a warning as to what may come of not resisting the rise of such governments in due time. But whereas any Holocaust memorial, wherever erected, may answer these two purposes, a German Holocaust memorial will, thirdly, be an exhibition of national shame. For the first time in history, a nation will embellish its capital with a monumental confession in stone or bronze of its misdeeds, of its forefathers as criminals! This, to my wonder and dismay, is never mentioned anywhere, has, as it were, been airbrushed from the PR photo. By whom? Obviously by a collective mind, unable or unwilling to entertain more than one thought at a time. Yet only the conflicting impulses, the feeling of the shame and *still* building what, among other things, proclaims that shame to eternity, gives the act its inspiring character. And if nothing else can bring those trivializers of German atonement face to face with that reality, then publicly voiced opposition to such a *Schandmal* ["monument of shame"] by whatever diehard, has to be welcomed. For if we build the thing without taking the *Schande* part into account, how on earth can we answer future German generations for saddling them with such un-asked-for heritage? What will we say to them? That we did it in a fit of absence of mind? Or that because once the idea had been suggested, nobody dared oppose it for fear of being viewed as a Nazi and antisemite?

Dear Jim, I suddenly realize that all the time I have been writing about this memorial and about the inability of people to acknowledge complexity and conflict of ideas in their minds, I have been fighting shy of agreeing to what you meant when you said, "You Germans are slaves." Must I not at long last admit that even now that we are rid of the outward marks of the vanquished and disabled, we still seem to be on the lookout for someone to tell us what to do, shunning the burden of autonomy that is the mark of the free?

Ignatz Bubis, the president of the Central Council of Jews in Germany, half pitying and half flattered, said in an interview with the *FAZ* (June 30, 1995) that before the planning of the said memorial had started, the parties involved had come to him and said, "Dear Mr. Bubis, you decide what memorial *you* want and we'll build it."

Think of that! As if Mr. Bubis or the Jews in general could relieve politicians and other German leading figures of their responsibility and accountability in a matter of such national weight!

I confess that it reminds me of the case of the great, old, sadly Hitler-smitten Knut Hamsun, who, after having been hunted down and harassed for years after 1945 by his unrelenting countrymen, at last came to answer every political question with "I'll say only what the police say is right."

If there is indeed a secret German wish to be rid, once and for all, of the moral complexities of a country that simply cannot be right, it found supreme expression in the publicly vented proposal last year to put up Mr. Bubis as candidate for the office of president of the Republic (which he graciously refused).

Yes, I'm weakening. My defences against your attacks on us Germans crumble. I might still successfully dispute you on certain points where I'm sure your fantasy is running wild — as when you indulge your pet idea that the Germans are secretly dreaming of revenging themselves on "Kanadier or Ami or Brit, if only they knew they could get away with it." I'll bet that's a projection of your most honourable feelings of Allied guilt, a projection onto Germans who feel nothing of the kind. Not even the neo-Nazis shouting "*Ausländer raus!*" [foreigners out!] are thinking of Americans, Canadians, or

Britons or of Frenchmen. But that's a minor point. What counts is that my daily reading of German newspapers and periodicals and listening to radio and TV, together with the impossibility of making my own voice heard, has led to a pessimism in matters German that is new to me and can now probably match yours.

Our oldest German demographic institute (Allensbach) has registered a steady increase of Left opinions since 1967 (or of German mainstream opinion steadily, imperceptibly moving to the Left), which shows that all the hubbub over the new rise of the Right in Germany is the fallacy I've always felt it was. People are alarmed at seeing others much further to the Right than formerly, precisely because their own movement to the Left has gone unnoticed. What used to be common sense and middle of the road by this shifting of the ground appears now as preposterous, impudent, Nazi, revisionist, and unconstitutional.

What, however, alarmed me was something nobody, not even the author of an article in the *FAZ*, Frau Noelle-Neumann, founder of the Allensbach Institute, is likely to have noticed. To ward off the predictable objection that the words *Left* and *Right* have long lost their meaning, the article also contained a two-columned table of typical views distinguishing Left and Right — and in neither column appeared the idea of freedom of expression or freedom of opinion, so dear to my understanding of democracy. But then what can you expect in a country in which there is no equivalent to the phrase "This a free country, you know," which I have come across ever so often in America.

Ah yes, those Angeli und Angli in your last letter. It is true, my Latin is nothing to write home about — owing to Hitler's quaint idea that English would be more important for me than Latin and then cutting my school career short altogether by starting a world war and relying on me to win it for him. But when daring to fiddle with Pope Gregory's (or as you kindly inform me, Venerable Bede's) "Non Angli sed Angeli" and making it "Non Anglus sed Angelus," I kept well within my little Latin, actually referring to A. J. P. Taylor as "Anglus" (Englishman) whom the crestfallen Germans of those postwar years considered a veritable "Angelus" (Angel) — a feeble joke, I admit, for which I hadn't sufficiently prepared you, dummkopf.

R.

August 21, 1995

Dear Richard,

Aha, dummkopf is it? Ahem. You are trying to pretend that your singular Latin was referring to the singular Taylor, not to the plural English. Let me remind you of your actual words, then: "non Anglus sed Angelus," as Pope Gregory had it. *Which of course he did not. Not only that, but the construction of your English sentence means that the Latin must refer to "my plural fellow Germans, proving them innocent," since it is the fellow Germans immediately preceding the Latin, and not Taylor.*

Speaking of angels, can you see my feet just touching the head of the pin as the wings of my argument keep me aloft? Do I feel your wingbeats beside me?

I have now discovered what may be the source of your impression that few Germans resisted, and that most of these were communists.

The source is German, Detlev J. K. Peukert, who reproduced in his book Volksgenossen und Gemeinschaftsfremde (Inside Nazi Germany) *a few figures for arrests of workers and others that make it seem as if the large majority of resisters were actually foreign workers. Few Germans were arrested, according to these statistics. But it appears that the definition for resisters that he uses is anyone whose arrest resulted in a judicial process. But Peter Hoffmann includes all arrests and imprisonments whether or not they included any judicial process. This is crucial, because the Gestapo had full power to arrest and to imprison people on suspicion without trial, so many of those arrested by the Gestapo probably did not appear in the Peukert figures. That may account for your belief that the communists were in the great majority among the resisters. Is this yet another example of German guilt displacing the truth about German resistance? Perhaps. It certainly is an example of the worth of such people as Hoffmann, relentless diggers for the documents.*

All the books that I have discovered that show the decency of ordinary people in Europe working under dangerous conditions to resist Nazis have been written by North Americans — Peter Hoffmann, Alfred de Zayas, Peter Hellman, Philip Hallie, Trudi Alexey, and others. I include myself, for Just Raoul. *It seems that the Europeans revel in guilt, especially the French and Germans, while the North Americans see more deeply, into the lives of the saints, if you will. We go to the record — documents, survivors, and so on, to show where kindness dispelled cru-*

elty. Why is that? Do we have a more positive attitude, so that we try to see the way out, to find the example that will help us to avoid the Hitlers in the future? I don't know.

One of the critical questions that you and I have failed to address is, Why is such guilt imposed on Germans born after the war ended? No such guilt is imposed on the Japanese, who after all had started their war even sooner, had bombed cities and massacred civilians. I think it has to do with a persistent, general dislike of Germans throughout Western society, a dislike I have certainly experienced following the publication of Other Losses.

I have for years been trying to understand why the French, Americans, and Germans have attacked Other Losses *and me personally with such savagery and deceit. Now I see that the critics are tortured by contradictory feelings. They are tempted to say of the victims of our atrocities, "So what? They were only Germans anyway. They got what they deserved." And they also say, "We are not Germans — we would never do such things." To hide the hypocrisy of the Western Great Leaders, they are forced to deny what they secretly approve. And this terrible conflict accounts for the many errors and the savagery of their attacks.*

Nazi crimes should never be demeaned, but new generations of Germans should not be loaded with guilt they do not deserve. Just as the world no longer blames the Jews or the Romans of today for the murder of Jesus Christ, no one in his right mind now should be blaming a twenty-four-year-old person for the sins of his grandfather. Since we are still doing this, since the Germans themselves are still doing this, we have to face the question, Why and how?

We have failed to come to grips with the tough question, Why such guilt? so we have necessarily failed to answer the much more important question, Can this be undone? And, What would the world look like if we succeeded?

Succeed in what? I suggest, succeed in removing government, the laws and courts and police, from the discussion of German history and Allied guilt since 1945. The totalitarian effort to make people believe and conform to norms of behaviour in Russia, in Germany, in medieval Europe and many other places failed in the end because freedom of discussion is essential to intelligence, and without intelligence, society can scarcely exist. Every effort that is made to suppress the discussion of German history, and especially of Allied guilt, bears the ominous stigma of the totalitarian; every lie told to defame the author of an uncomfortable truth is a defamation of the whole society. The lies, propaganda, suppressions, threats of prosecution, and so on are like termites in a cottage, chewing away bit by bit at the structure until it is a hollowed shell with no strength left, ready to fall at the first strain. That was the U.S.S.R. in the 1980s. The termites are always at work.

What would you and I like to see happen now? What would I like to see happen? What would be good for Germany, in my opinion? Nervy questions, of course, but we can learn from recent history. There are many examples in the past sixty years of how political parties newly in power have dealt with past internal enemies of the state. The Nazis in 1933-39 brought ruin to millions of Germans, and so did the communists in the U.S.S.R. in the 1920s and 1930s. Both Germany and Russia were torn apart by the officially sponsored and violent vengeance taken against communists, fascists, bourgeois, imperialists, Jews, clergy, royalists, and so on. But even under the relatively benign Western democracies, there was tremendous vengeance that damaged the work of education and reconciliation.

Timothy Garton Ash has written that the experience in Germany after reunification shows that the law rarely produces justice. "Since the leaders [of the GDR] are often old and sick, and the evidence flawed, you end up with a farce like the Honecker trial.... Administrative screenings and purges are almost invariably unjust.... What is most effective of all however, is simply information, knowledge, and — dare one say? — truth. This is what West Germany did so well (though after a very slow start) about Nazis, and what united Germany has done best about its communist legacy." Ash goes on to dismiss the effectiveness of officially sponsored public agencies, because they are "invariably constrained by political considerations."

"Best of all," Ash writes,

is giving individual citizens the opportunity to confront, preferably in private, their own pasts. This is where the opening of the Stasi files has been in my view, exemplary. It is painful. It often carries a very high personal cost: the discovery that a dear friend, even a husband or brother, has informed on you. It has led to painful confrontations all over East Germany in the last few years. But it has not, as critics feared, torn East German society apart. It has, for many, many people, brought a sense of catharsis, resolution, the feeling of a chapter closed which enables them to go forward to another.... It is on this basis, individually, privately, slowly, that people actually do 'come to terms with,' or even 'overcome' the past.

The same is true of reconciliation between peoples: governments can help to create the right conditions, but what matters, ultimately, are the feelings and experiences of individual men and women, which governments can neither force nor direct.[40]

These are wise words. One might add that Ash is telling us to practice the virtues of the society that survived while others came crashing down. He is preaching the virtues of (German) democracy — the use of the individual consciences in lieu of the forced obedience of the authoritarian state, to discuss instead of dictate, to convince instead of convict.

I am fascinated by your news of the proposal to construct a memorial in Berlin to the Jewish victims of Hitler. There is more than national significance in this memorial because, as you say, this would be the only memorial in the world erected by a whole people in commemoration of their own shame. In London, Paris, Ottawa, Washington, and Moscow are thousands of monuments to the glories of the nation's conquests. We have yet to see in London a monument to the atrocities committed by the British against the Boers, there is none in Paris admitting the crimes of La Patrie *against the Vietnamese or the Algerians, none in Ottawa to record the suppression of native and Métis rights on the Canadian prairies, nothing in Washington to memorialize the aggression of the Americans against a whole continent of nations from east to west, and nothing in Moscow to denounce the crimes of the czars or communists against Eastern Europeans or the indigenous peoples conquered over centuries between Old Russia and the Pacific.*

If we can agree for the moment that in our era what we mean by a country, or a people, such as the Germans or the English or the Canadians, consists mainly of the nation-state, and the culture, we see that the proposed monument rebukes the nation-state of the Germans. After all, it was to serve the nation-state — das Reich — *that the war was made on the U.S.S.R., and the subject peoples murdered. It was the nation-state and not the culture that was abolished in 1945. All the criminals tried and hanged at Nuremberg and later were employees of that pitiless machine.*

Germany today is the result of the survival of a culture, not of a form of government. It was impossible for the Allies to abolish German culture, although they went far toward it. German culture survived, and when it

40 Timothy Garton Ash in the *New York Review of Books*, July 13, 1995: 21.

was allowed once again to express itself in a government, the reborn state displayed no trace of fascism, kaiserism, imperial designs in the east of Europe, or any other of the major aggressive characteristics of German governments before 1945. Germans today have no sense of unity deriving from a long line of emperors, as in Japan, or from love of the Royal Family, as in England, or from devotion to the Constitution, as in the U.S. After 1945, the government was divided in four and handed to aliens, the borders shrank terribly, the constitution changed, the administrators changed, the name of the parliament changed, the method of choosing the rulers changed — everything changed in the nation-state, but little else. The language did not change, or any other aspect of culture. The German people have survived because of their language, music, literature, education, medicine, philosophy, science, engineering, Christian religion, their characteristic orderliness, hard work, cleanliness, and so on. As for Canada, it has scarcely any unity — it is a government in search of a country. Whereas you for so many years were a country in search of a government.

One of the results today has been to make Germany unique. It is the first big non-nationalistic nation-state in the world, excepting perhaps Canada. In a world of heavily armed, pugnacious world-states, Germany has no army capable of aggression, or even of self-defence. She has forsworn expansion, she is incapable of defence, and yet she is not isolated. On the contrary, she lives by exports and imports. Germany is a world struggling to be born, a people locked inside borders set by others. It is a state formed by the will of others, mainly to implement the economic policies of its people. You have announced your guilt. And now you abjure pride. Your state is ending, and will probably change into a province of Europe, but for now you must live inside its remains like a chrysalis awaiting its next mode of being.

This is important to me, because I have tried to write something sensible and useful on the subject of preventing aggression by nation-states, and have failed. I don't think anything can prevent it except the reduction of the nation-state. And that avoids the issue because the cause is not in our states, Horatio, but in ourselves. Human beings are aggressive, even in the womb, so nothing will end aggression until human beings voluntarily relinquish it as a matter of policy. But we are already seeing a completely new expression of the natural human aversion to collective violence. By this I mean of course the abandonment of weapons of large-scale aggression by nation-states, with the destruction of nuclear arsenals by the U.S. and Russia.

This is inevitably going to mean a huge change in the nation-states. Since the prime characteristic in the success of the nation-state has always been that it spread political peace over a wide area in which people immediately began to grow prosperous through trade, the slow spread of international peace throughout the world since 1945 has meant that the nation-state has lost part of its function. International trade has risen as never before in history; fewer and fewer people per capita are at risk of war.

The astounding destructiveness of the Second World War and the arrival of atomic weapons have largely eliminated the desire among nation-states to search for large-scale gain by large-scale means. Since peoples, even the most independent and isolated, such as the Japanese, no longer feel sufficient unto themselves in matters of trade but search restlessly around the world for innovation, prosperity, profit, delight, and education, the function of the nation-state as the prospering pacifier has diminished. It is now seen not as the pacifier of internal matters, or even as that perversion of itself, the means to imperial gain, but simply as an internal regulator, a large-scale charitable organization, an efficient administrator of those parts of the nation's life that cannot yet be administered so well by private means. And that, it seems to me, is Germany. And perhaps Canada.

What is already starting to replace nation-states is communities of interest. By interest, I mean cultural, religious, and economic groups. The Roman Catholic Church and the Hudson's Bay Company are two examples from history of long-lived, successful communities of interest. Cultural groupings that have survived are the Scots and the Jews in diaspora. And there are hybrids such as the British Commonwealth of nations that combine elements of all three.

Your country and mine, very similar in many ways, are further along this inevitable path than any others, as far as I can tell. In both Germany and Canada, national policy is turned inward, on national problems, of helping the people, of redistributing wealth — all the characteristics of the twentieth century welfare state. We contribute to the UN and to international peacekeeping (except Germany gives money, not yet troops) and we do not seek conquests abroad. In comparison with all the other democracies, Canadians are low in pride — one might almost say that the one thing we are proud of is our humility. Many Germans are ashamed of their country's past, and Canada too is poisoned by a history that is incurable but not terminal. We too have forsworn the atomic bomb, which we could have built fifty years ago. We too formed the frontier against the

Soviets for fifty years, and would have been among the very first victims of war; we too are incapable of self-defence, we have no imperialist ambitions, are international, must exist by export and import, and so on. We, like you, want our nation-state to administer efficiently essential internal affairs, not to adventure abroad as in the Falkland Islands, Vietnam, Algeria, Afghanistan, and so on.

If we can turn these letters into a successful book, and if it has any influence on people, it will help to liberate Germans. But people in Germany and elsewhere will want to know, What are the dangers in this? So I leave you with a question: Do the Germans as a nation, as a cultural group, or as communities of interest present more of a threat of aggression than other people in the world?

J.

September 15, 1995

Dear Jim,

I'm glad that your new book is on its way now and definitely to be presented at the Frankfurt book fair — and also, of course, that this means we'll be seeing each other soon. I think the relief of having *Crimes and Mercies* (at least in the German version) safely launched shows in your August letter. A certain peace of mind seems to have descended on you, allowing you to take wide views and concentrate on really big points. It is also — for the first time, I believe — a letter that contains almost no criticism of Germany. On the contrary, it puts Germany (alongside Canada) in a very special and positive bracket. That's a reversal of fronts I'll have to come to terms with. After all, *my* last letter ended on a note of deep pessimism. Was that — in a twisted way — the cause of your crossing over? Did you feel free to come down in favour of Germany the very moment I felt so bitter about her?

Be that as it may, your idea that the nation-state is on its way out has certainly been very much in the air for some time. But while some people would agree with you that it has been the root of all past and present political evil and would welcome its demise, others would rather stem the tide, because they fear the replacement of the nation-state by remote super-organizations, multi-cultural chaos, and petty quarrels flaring up at the lower end of regions and provinces. Your letter in fact winds up with doubts whether aggression, deprived of its nationalist hovel, will not rear its head in other places. I must confess I always experience a certain vertigo when asked to consider "ultimate" questions of this kind. I feel more at home on a one-off level.

I do believe that Germany is more advanced than most other countries in discarding nationalism. And a good thing too. It's also true that there is a strong groundswell in Germany toward going the whole hog and doing away altogether with the nation-state and its "trappings" such as guarded borders, army, police, government, foreign policy, sovereignty, flag, anthem, national monuments, cultural and language unity. Others are wary of this tendency toward wholesale atomization and anarchy. They still like to belong to traditional political tangibles, to a governable body politic they can feel protected by and at home in. They are not (yet) convinced that the baby nation-state should be thrown out with the dirty bathwater of nationalism. As for myself, I can see and even feel the attraction of getting rid of what the Germans were never really good at. But what if the Germans now debunking the nation-state do get what they like and then perhaps don't like what they get (having merely swapped one extremism and short-sightedness for another)?

This doesn't mean that I'm not moved by your bold idea of our two countries providing a pattern of how nations should confront the world of today and tomorrow. But does the erection of a Holocaust monument in Berlin really rebuke the nation-state of the Germans? It does rebuke what elsewhere has been typical of nation-states: their pride of their forefathers and forgers of that politically exclusive home, of their conquering heroes, even of their monsters like Ivan the Terrible, Henry VIII, or Napoleon. But there is always a dialectic in the destruction of something. Luther seemed to destroy the Church, but as has been said with some justice, he thereby gave an institution possibly on its way out a new lease on life — even in its papist form. It may surprise you that several of the critics of the Berlin monument and other German attempts at expiation accuse the Germans of (mis)using their victims as a means for establishing a much coveted new national identity. If for a moment one ignores the meanness of giving the Germans no credit for whatever they do, there is perhaps more than a grain of truth in this. The German nation-state is so bound up with Hitler's Nazism that renouncing

Hitler by building a monument to the memory of his victims can be seen as the only way left to save it.

But I am of course with you in calling public attention to what makes Germany positively unique today — not at all in order to put others down, and not in an attempt to bury German sins, but because I think that human beings can't keep up the good fight without some recognition of the good in them by others and by themselves. I should in fact like my countrymen to be modestly proud of the right things instead of the wrong — as they often were at other times, and if that strengthens their feeling of being a nation worth belonging to, I welcome that.

We should admit, however, that the world, and Germany herself, has had to suffer overmuch in the process of German improvement and also that things beyond German wish and will have contributed to what we can now congratulate her on. The context of world politics has changed — fundamentally so, and present dangers arise very much from countries not yet able or willing to acknowledge this. Not only the experience of the Second World War and the advent of the A-bomb have "largely eliminated the desire among nation states to search for large-scale gain by large-scale means" (James Bacque). It's also a new truth and fact that the size of countries, i.e., land gains, including colonies, do no longer count for much in terms of national well-being.

The mainly agricultural idea of *Lebensraum* has lost its seductive power. Recent history teaches that any nation trying to go it alone is bound to find itself sooner or later at the bottom. Not even the possession of big oil fields ensures ascendancy over others any longer, not to speak of a people's happiness, as the OPEC states found out to their surprise.

Thanks for the *New Yorker* (August 14, 1995) with the "Letter from Germany: Politics of Memory" by Jane Kramer, which has arrived this morning. But I'm afraid I had to step outside and inhale some fresh autumn air after I had finished reading. This cloying, stifling stuff, drawn out over seventeen pages, was too much for me. I wonder if ever the time will come that writers of this mean and smirking bent will suddenly see their own portrait emerging from such texts, see themselves from the outside — this vain cocksureness and public posturing, these facile witticisms in the face of a nation shown wriggling on the pin of its past (plus a few side kicks at the neighbouring Poles). It is obvious that all the time she gleefully parades German complexities, pitfalls, ambiguities, and confusions, we are invited to share her super-superiority over her subject, her easy, though — unfortunately — unrevealed, knowledge of what these damn Germans *really* ought to be doing. Would it come as a shock to her to see herself for once through my eyes? Would she blush? I hope so.

Which, of course, reminds me of your question, "Why is such guilt imposed on Germans born after the war ended?" But you see, it isn't. The word *guilt* isn't used in this context. It would indeed be too absurd, unless one believed in collective guilt, which logically would even include German Jews. The word that is considered correct to apply to young Germans is *Haftung* or "liability." *Responsibility* is another evasive term used, which shares with guilt and liability the trait of unrelievable burden, of duty to somebody who forever threatens to be knocking on your door producing an IOU with an unspecified sum on it.

And why that?

Because it is said to be impossible for the victims, the bereaved, and their friends to see things in a different light, to draw a line, to admit a fresh start. This has much to do with the peculiar nature of collective entities, of nations, institutions, firms, and so on. How can you be generous, forgiving in the name of untold others toward people, however young, calling themselves Germans? How dare you speak in the name of your fellow beings? It is a standard saying on the part of the Jews that only their dead might forgive. If this testifies to the still-insurmountable sorrow and pain of the living, I am not saying a word against it, I can only bow my head. But if it is advanced as a logical argument, it's inadmissable. For it only raises the question it is meant to silence. If only the dead were entitled to offer forgiveness, they would by the same token be the only ones in a position to refuse it.

Dear Jim, these are sad and heavy things to speak about. But I feel one has to tackle them. We have to think and talk about them courageously for the very reason that they involve millions upon millions of young Germans who in their several ways will decide what Germany is going to be like in the next millennium. And I simply can't believe, and you seem to be with me here, that the best way to approach them is to talk of burdens and duties and liabilities instead of appealing to their freedom, their high spirits, and compassion, leaving it to them to decide what to do with the sins and the guilt of their forefathers. As we inevitably must anyway eventually.

Do the Germans, you ask at the end of your letter, present more of a threat of aggression than other people in the world?

I don't think so. Nothing I can see points that way, and you have confirmed it in that last letter of yours. Germany has no nuclear potential, and it has an enormous and rising rate of conscientious objectors to military service. This year the number is most likely to top 170,000 out of 363,774. Germany is quietly content to have achieved reunification with its torn-off Soviet-ruled part, it has solemnly renounced all foreign policy that might interfere with the happiness of its neighbours, it spends more billions of its currency than any other of its partners to make a United Europe work, it is hosting far more refugees than any other country not immediately adjacent to the scenes of war or other disaster, and no country in history has done more to come to terms with its evil past and its victims. I dare say that to most Germans the idea that Germany, of all nations, should be willing and able to start another war or threaten its neighbours with aggression sounds pretty absurd. I said something to that effect in an earlier letter. But the idea still haunts you — and other people. The question most pressing for me is, Why is that? How is that to be explained?

Looking for an answer, I have hit on three possibilities:

- There simply is this irrational hatred of a nation neither small enough to ignore nor big enough to really fear, and how better to justify this hatred but by convincing yourself that you're still dealing with mankind's archenemy?
- Thinking about what Germans were capable of in the past, the people of the world, imagining themselves in the shoes of Germans today, feel what they would feel and do if they were them. No matter what they are told, in their heart of hearts they can't believe that German reactions to 1945 can be that different from what their own would be.
- At the back of their minds everybody knows well enough who the aggressive and threatening nations of today's world really are (or where at least the potential for new super-bullies lies). As nothing, or nothing short of a nuclear world war, could possibly stop *them*, they are being treated with utmost caution, while the feeling of resentment going with such restraint seeks refuge in the rites of burning the familiar old Guy.

You take your pick. There is still the more general question of why Germans are universally detested and hated (as you maintain). I'm not exactly keen on addressing this question. Many non-Germans do not admit the presupposition, and where does that then leave me? Another reason is that at one level the answer is so obvious — and painful. There is also the general futility of probing in public for answers to fundamental questions about yourself or your nation. On the whole I think people prefer other people to be who they are instead of being forced to listen to their worrying about who they may be. For, as Goethe said, "How canst thou know thyself and *be* at the same time?"

I think Do right and fear no man is still good advice, basically. If the German starting position for doing right is far behind others, well, that's to be reckoned with; but can it be helped?

R.

November 17, 1995

Dear Richard,

Your remark about Goethe really lit me up because he is saying something that worried me when I was a young man trying to decide what to do with my life. I wanted to write, but I did not want to be a writer because I thought I would have to observe others and at the same time live among them, observe myself, and be myself. I hated the idea of deliberately turning myself into an observer of all I was and did because it would divide my nature. I thought it would make me feel sick. And yes, sometimes it does.

And I guess you and I are both doing that on a large scale by trying to observe and describe what we are so much a part of. A bit like a fish trying to analyze the chemical composition of water.

So maybe observing you from outside the fishbowl, I can help you find an answer to your question about the Holocaust memorial. You ask if the construction of a Holocaust memorial in Berlin rebukes your nation-state, and I reply, "Of course it does. If it does not, it loses half its point, because the atrocity was committed by the top leaders of the nation-state of Germany in the 1940s." One of the constraints on my (formerly) strong Canadian nationalism was the realization of Canada's shameful treatment of minorities in our power — the aborigines, for centuries, and, briefly, Ukraine before the First World War, Germany during the First World War, the Italians and Japanese during the Second World War.

No physical monument to their suffering under various Canadian administrations has ever been erected, but most of their history has been told by now, so I know where my pride in Canada ends and where my sense of outrage begins — outrage at the cynical betrayal of our civilizing ideals by the leaders of our…nation-state!

This process of historical truth telling has gone so far in Canada that I can say I do not believe any significant history is now being hidden. And much is being rectified. Injustices against the aborigines are slowly being abolished or compensated where possible, apologies are offered, land restored. There is no doubt that all of us are better for this process, and I am sure the same applies in Germany.

However, I find it hard to believe that some Germans are using their victims as one way to help re-establish a German identity. How convoluted can you get? Anyone with strong nationalist/revival feelings, such as, say, the neo-Nazis, automatically rejects evidence of his country's sins a priori. As for the "guilt" now being imposed on young Germans: you say it isn't really guilt but Haftung, *liability. As you correctly point out,* Haftung *is a liability that anyone can collect at any time, virtually at will. And this* Haftung *is very convenient for anyone who wants to make Germans bow their heads and get out of the way.*

All this leads to your powerful argument about forgiveness. Many of the survivors are now saying, "Only our dead could forgive." But as you say, "If only the dead were entitled to forgive, they would by the same token be the only ones entitled to refuse it." Touché.

Your defence of Germany's peaceful intentions now does not convince me, except the observation about the conscientious objectors, which is very convincing. My question to you was not based on current events but was rather a Pavlovian response created by the events of the twentieth century before 1945. Therefore, I welcome what you say about the immense objections to military service registered by young Germans. Bravo to them. And I shall suggest to Lord Alfred[41], that we should now make it a basic human right that all citizens be exempt from military service. Only volunteers should staff armies in the future.

Alfred drove me from Heidelberg to Göttingen yesterday (October 20), where he was to give a lecture on Germany at the university. He practiced

41 Bacque's friend Alfred de Zayas, senior legal counsel to the UN High Commission for Human Rights in Geneva.

on me for two hours at 170 kph. It was a magnificent exposé of a country he knows well, as he drove to a city he loves, Göttingen, where he took his doctorate in German history. (That's where I am writing this part of my letter.)

I was impressed not just by his ability to navigate the autobahn at 170 kph while delivering an impassioned lecture, but because he expressed so well his long and harsh experience with the truth, one that parallels my own. Like him, I have been horrified to find a cultured rich European nation of eighty million people who were self-loathing, self-abusing, masochistic to the point that the only national feeling that joins them is their shame.

It seems that everything but a frantic philistinism is beyond the Germans now. They are so disgusted with themselves that they do not even want to reproduce themselves. The German birth rate is well below the death rate, as it has been for years, while among all of Germany's neighbours, including countries even more crowded than Germany, the birth rate still exceeds the death rate. If this phenomenon is not largely caused by the self-hatred of Germans, I don't know what the cause could be — excessive materialism? — because, after all, Germany is the most prosperous of all these countries and not the most crowded.[42]

To reveal the hidden truth about events through documents and witnesses is not enough to make much difference to history, as Alfred and I have found. A greater mysterious process is at work, the work of feeling and myth, which may annul truth and establish error. All understanding of society must also include an understanding of the processes of feeling and will, of mythmaking and truth telling, and how these processes of feeling and will often overrule the facts, as they do in Germany today.

---

42 Sample of some European countries' birth/death rate

Country	1975		1989	
	Births	Deaths	Births	Deaths
Austria	NA	NA	89,000	83,000
France	743,000	559,000	765,000	529,000
Germany (West)	601,000	749,000	880,000	903,000
Netherlands	NA	NA	189,000	129,000
Poland	644,000	297,000	563,000	381,000
UK	603,000	583,000	777,000	NA

Sources: *UN Demographic Yearbook* 1992, New York 1994, and Mitchell, *European Historical Statistics* London, 1981.

That the truth Alfred and I have told is so much ignored or resisted in the west-of-Aachen is of course inevitable, we see, because these were Allied crimes and errors, and no one wants to admit his errors and sins. This is an inevitable truth about human nature, one thinks, but the moment we cross the Rhine into Germany, we find that this apparently inescapable truth is completely reversed.

I think that at last I have come to a small useful conclusion about this guilt of yours that has so preoccupied me in these letters. It was prompted in part by your clear analysis (your letter of April 24, 1994) of German atonement and the establishment becoming drunk on their own virtue. It seems to me that the guilt is both real and chimerical, like a religion. This guilt religion has been defined, taught, and imposed by the state or another superior power, like most religions. It is so widely believed that it has been approved by the Bundestag as part of the official religion of Germany, to be defended by punitive laws that threaten anyone who challenges it.

Yet the need for punitive measures shows at the same time that the guilt religion is not widely believed, or else it would not have to be imposed and maintained by force. Do you have a law imposing a jail sentence on anyone who says that the sun revolves around the earth? Ridiculous, you say, but it is a fair analogy, because the earth's orbit was an angrily disputed religious point for centuries. The guilt has both the status and the weakness of a religion. And we all know what happened when a tough German last opposed an official religion. There is the danger. Legislation cannot replace education; persuasion is better than prison.

Consider: if in 1939, most Germans had been true followers of the then-prevalent official religion, Christianity, they would have been forbidden to harm their neighbours, bound to love God and their fellow man, and to turn the other cheek to their enemies. If they had done that, it would have been impossible for the Nazis to persuade Germany to attack her neighbours and slaughter so many civilians during the war. For most Germans, duty to the Fatherland in 1939 or the Fuehrer oath were far more important than their love of God and of each other and Christ's teachings. The Germans' nominal belief in Christianity was swept aside like a sand castle by a flood during the cataclysmic events after 1938. If such a strong, appealing, enduring, widespread religion as Christianity could be so easily ignored, how much more easily may the German guilt of today be swept aside by some new dangerous demagogue.

We are already seeing some of the evil effects of this guilt religion in the destruction of freedoms that the Allies brought to Germany after 1945.

Germany's form of democracy is accompanied by, and harshly enforces, this guilt religion that destroys one of the fundamentals of democracy, free speech. There is nothing in the U.S. to compare with the laws against the Auschwitz-lie, or the Radikalenerlass *rules, or the rough laws against defaming the memory of the dead. No, the Americans practice what they preach — they allow revisionist opinions to be expressed, because they believe in free speech. Preaching humbug endangers no one; suppression endangers everyone. And that this is also believed in the rest of Europe is shown by the fact that your* Radikalenerlass *was recently condemned by the European court at Strasbourg.*[43]

Large stretches of post war German history are being denied and suppressed today, though these were openly discussed by British, Americans, and Germans in the past. In the Swiss Parliament in March 1949, and then again in his Erinnerungen *(memoir), Konrad Adenauer described the crimes committed by the Allies against the Germans in the following words: "Crimes have been committed that can take their place beside those committed by the Nazis." (Original German reads:* Es sind Untaten verübt worden, die sich den von den deutschen Nationalsozialisten verübten Untaten würdig an die Seite stellen.*)*[44] *These words were pronounced on foreign soil to an important foreign audience, and certainly overheard by the Americans, British, French, and Soviets, all of whom were guilty, and therefore accused. Yet the British, Americans, and French permitted Adenauer to take over as chancellor of West Germany soon thereafter. I suggest that it would be absolutely impossible for a German writer to get such a comparison published in a mainstream journal or TV show today.*

---

43 The *Radikalenerlass.* In 1972 Chancellor Willy Brandt and the Chiefs of the German *Laenders* agreed on rules for keeping adherents of extremist parties ("enemies of the constitution"), mainly communists, but also neo-Nazis, out of the state service. Since in Germany many jobs are part of the state service (teachers, railway-, post-officials and others), this concerned a large number of people. A decision of the European Court of Human Rights favoured a German teacher who had been removed from her job because she had been a functionary of the communist DKP. The court is an emanation of the 40 nations composing the Council of Europe and is not to be confused with the European Court of Justice, which is the judicial branch of the European Union. The teacher was reinstated.

44 Adenauer, *Erinnerungen,* Deutsche Verlags-Anstalt, Stuttgart, Band I, 1965, p. 186.

For instance, there was an article in the European Magazine *recently (October 1995) about another chancellor, Helmut Schmidt, which illustrates the point. Adenauer in 1949 quite openly compared Allied crimes to Nazi crimes, but today Helmut Schmidt is publicly insulted when he states that he knew nothing of German crimes against Russian civilians during his service on the Eastern Front. The writer, Dalbert Hallenstein, quotes the clear statement by Schmidt that he knew absolutely nothing of "the annihilation of Russian soldiers, of civilians or of the Jews. I only found out after the war"; and Hallenstein comments, "One is forced to wonder if there was a survival instinct, a sort of Stockholm syndrome, at work in him to avoid all knowledge of these horrors in order not to go insane." The writer clearly impugns Schmidt's statement that he did not know about these things. How could Schmidt know without knowing? How could he not know while knowing? What evidence does Hallenstein have for implying that Schmidt is a liar? He should either produce the evidence, or apologize, like a good German.*

So here is Schmidt, undoubtedly an honourable man, subject to this sneer in a major European paper. But does he sue for libel? Not a chance. He simply accepts it as so many Germans do, as if it were deserved. And this is the same Schmidt who, you said in yours of December 7, 1993, was an example of Germans who have the "manly ideal."

Three of the most expert German historians of the age recently read my new book Crimes and Mercies, *and all were astonished to discover that Adenauer had said there were six million dead among the refugees alone. Not one of them could at first believe it was true. Alfred de Zayas, historian of the post-war expulsions of Germans and Otto Kimminich, who has also written about the expulsions, did not know this fact until I revealed it to them. And when the historian Ernst Nolte read these passages in my book in his study in Berlin, he immediately opened his own copy of Adenauer's memoir, found the passages, read them over, and said, "It is amazing what one could say in those days [the 1940s and 1950s] and one cannot say now."*

We read that the Germans of today are the first good Europeans, but isn't that motivated in part by their self-hatred? Isn't it that they think it is better to be European than German? But then it also seems that for many Germans these questions of guilt and becoming Europeans are no longer very important.

I asked a young German who had been canoeing in Canada if he felt guilty and he said, "Of course not." I asked him if he felt like a European, and he seemed indifferent. "Do you identify with Germany?" I asked, and he said, "No, with my region. I am a Hamburg man. Why should I identify with a Bavarian?" "Because you both speak German," I said, and he said, "Yes, but I speak English as well." He explained that he was concerned with his family and his job as well as his region. I got the impression that everything else was a bit unreal to him.

Today in Germany, it seems to me, these questions of guilt and Europeanness are the concerns of the politicians much more than of the people. And isn't that more or less what A. J. P. Taylor said about not wanting his country to take part in the idiocy of striving after greatness and domination? There is a common sense in that which cancels the glory-mongering of the high men. Maybe this is the wisdom of aversion, the recognition that everyday lives are much more important than the lofty questions that animated Hitler, Lenin, and the others and that lead so often to destruction.

Germany today has been ironically called die Canossa-Republik, *by Leonard Meri, the president of Estonia, because it is constantly doing penance for its sins, like the Emperor Henry IV who stood barefoot in the snow before Pope Gregory VII at Canossa in 1077.*[45]

But Meri went beyond irony in his speech about Germany. He invited the Germans of Estonia to return. Doing that, he showed that the Christian message is valid today and can be carried out even by those who suffered dreadfully from Hitler. Estonia was precariously independent in August 1939, when a secret protocol was struck between Hitler's foreign minister, Ribbentrop, and Stalin's foreign minister, Molotov. In public, Germany and the U.S.S.R. allied themselves, which relieved Hitler of the danger of a two-front war, while guaranteeing Germany an ally in the attack on Poland. In a secret protocol, Hitler agreed that Stalin could take over Estonia and half of Latvia, countries that had strong German ties, and a significant German presence, i.e., many citizens of German ancestry. This was a cynical, barbarous arrangement, the first step in the long, disastrous oppression of Estonia by the Soviets, which lasted over fifty years.

At the end of the war, many German-origin Estonians fled before the Red Army as it returned to Estonia; a few more were expelled after the

---

45 Lexicographers, please note: the metaphor *die Canossa Republik* was invented
   by Paul Boytinck of Lewisburg, Pennsylvania, who first uttered it to Alfred
   de Zayas and me at lunch in the garden at 422 Heath Street in Toronto,
   March 1995. De Zayas said he would use the catchy phrase and so he did, in
   a speech in Berlin two weeks later, where it was widely reported. Meri
   presumably saw it in that newspaper report.

war. These are the Germans who have now been invited to return by the president. This is the first time that any expelled Germans have in effect been forgiven by a country betrayed and oppressed by the Germans, the first time that any expellees have been invited to return to their former homeland, and yet this major speech caused hardly any reaction in the German media. One of the journals of the expellees, Ostpreussenblatt *of Hamburg, of course reported it, and to its credit* Die Welt *carried a brief report and an editorial, but to my knowledge, even weeks after this tremendous act of forgiveness, no other German paper and no TV or radio network made anything of it.*

I find this incredible. Is this another case of Germans unable to forgive themselves, even though they are forgiven by their (former) victims?

Can it be that while many Germans no longer care to be forgiven, official Germany is afraid of it — just as the Social Democrats were afraid of seeing Germany united?

Dishonest rewriting of history has been going on for forty years, not only in Germany but elsewhere, to load guilt on the innocent. In Holland, France, the U.S. and Canada, there is hardly any understanding at all between the generation that lived through the events and the younger ones, who have been taught incompletely about them. I recently encountered a cynicism and narrowness of view among some young Dutch people that staggered me. This was at a friendly dinner in Geneva. Someone referred to the fiftieth anniversary of the war's end, which had recently been celebrated in Holland. Three young Dutch people were there, aged thirty-six, thirty, and about twenty-five, all university educated.

One of them said she disagreed with the celebrations. I said it was wonderful to celebrate the liberation of their country. She said the Dutch were very guilty because they had handed their Jews over to the Nazis. I said that the celebrations were important because they honoured the brave soldiers who had ended all that horror. Freedom and joy had arrived on the Canadian tanks — hadn't she seen the films of Dutch people jumping up onto the tanks of the First Canadian Army that liberated the country? She said angrily that the people were guilty. By now I was shouting at her, and she was in a cold rage. She had to ask me to stop shouting, so I apologized (like a good German) and things grew quieter. But clearly there was an unreconciled difference between us: she had been made to feel guilty, though she was not even alive at the time. Of course I felt virtuous, though I had never worn an Allied uniform. But the worst of it is that this illustrates once again that the teaching of recent history is so biased now that many people view the Second World War as only a backdrop to the Holocaust.

I have also encountered the same sort of thing in France, a widespread guilt, though the French people did much to save refugees during the war, under the most difficult conditions. One reads of the terrible roundups the Germans conducted, notably at the Vel d'Hiver *in Paris in 1942. Before the roundup there were about twenty-eight thousand Jewish names on police lists in Paris, but when the roundup actually occurred, about fifteen thousand of these had been warned in time and had escaped. Undoubtedly, many must have been warned by French police.*

Most of the Jews seized and deported by the Nazis in France were refugees who had arrived in France before the conquest. They were easy to round up because most of them were already in internment camps such as Gurs, in the southwest, and they lacked French citizenship papers. But the Jews of French citizenship were a far different story. "There were enormous numbers of people helping the Jews," said Gilbert Lesage, a French Quaker, when I interviewed him in Paris in September 1989 at the Centre de Documentation Juive Contemporaine. *The French were able to save about 87 per cent of their fellow citizens, while about 40 per cent of the refugees were deported to the east.[46]*

But the stories of heroic saviours like Raoul Laporterie of Grenade and André Trocmé of Le-Chambon-sur-Lignon went untold for forty years, except at Yad Vashem in Israel, where they are honoured. Nothing was known of them in France until North Americans such as Philip Hallie, Peter Hellman, Trudi Alexy and I came along to tell their stories for the first time.

Most of this is strange and even depressing stuff for a Canadian to learn, I assure you. But I think maybe I have learned something else from our letters, from my week in Germany with you, and my two-week tour.

I have learned from your realism that is never cynical, from your historical knowledge that is rarely gloomy, your creative energy that is never facile optimism, and above all your clearheadedness. In the necessary guilt of Germany for a war in which you shared yourself, there is also, I think, a necessary result. This will be a nation without nationalism, wise with the wisdom of aversion to evil. This predicts a people who will be defined not by borders or armies, not by threat, compulsion, or lying diplomacy, but by the persuasions and temptations of culture, art, generous politics, creative trade.

The German devotion to Europe, the polylingualism of your country, the generous retrieval of the impoverished eastern third of your country,

---

46 James Bacque, *Just Raoul,* Toronto, Stoddart Publishing Co. 1991, 174.

your international trade, the hundreds of billions of marks you have paid in reparations and are still paying to Hitler's victims, the amazing lack of bitterness toward your vengeful conquerors — are all signs of this. Scarcely an ex-PoW among the thousands who wrote to me and whom I interviewed after Other Losses, *has ever expressed hatred of the Allies for the atrocities they committed against Germans in 1945 to 1950 or advocated revenge.*

In the name of righteousness (or vengeance), the governments of Canada and the U.S. harass citizens whom they know committed no war crimes, but no one in Germany has ever suggested that the perpetrators of the crimes against Germans should be brought to justice. Yet if the Nuremberg rules were applied to them, many thousands of war criminals would be tried. You are ignoring our evil while accepting your own. In this, you are definitely far different from us.

The most you wish is that the historical record be set straight by truth; some of you even dislike this process because it reminds you of your guilt, or seems to detract from the guilt on which you pride yourselves, unite yourselves. You maintain a faith in us that we have lost in you. From you and your nation I have learned a lot. Revenge is waste.

Well, Richard, it looks as if we are getting near the end of this voyage. We may come to success or grief — who knows? All we can do, you and I, is to keep the logbook clearly and hope to live to the end of the voyage, sure of where we were, but with only a child's perception of what it is we see around us now.

Thank you, dear enemy.

J.

February 9, 1996

Dear Jim,

We may be getting near the end of our voyage, all right, but we're not quite there, I think. When I got to the point in your last letter where you asked, "Is this another case of Germans unable to forgive themselves...?" I wondered what you would make of the very latest craze in German self-denial, i.e., the success of *Hitler's Willing Executioners* by one Daniel Goldhagen.

The first thing I noted with regard to this book was the almost unanimous rejection of it by German, American, Canadian, and British historians/critics (including Jews). Well, I thought, that's that. Meanwhile, however, the scene has completely changed. The sheer impact of media attention, especially after the German translation was out, roused the German atonement camp, who are resolved to applaud anything, however dubious, that helps to keep the flame of German remorse and expiation burning. Those who considered the book a monstrous offence against fundamental rules of the historian's trade, have to their consternation now to grapple not with Goldhagen but with the danger of being shoved into the corner of right-wing German insensitivity.

I have to admit that by now Goldhagen has won. By virtue of his book's combination of a show of scholarship with excessively repetitive propaganda, anything one may say against it will appear as mere nitpicking.

His central thesis is that the Germans had for centuries been more antisemitic than comparable societies, that their antisemitism was of a particularly nasty kind in being "eliminationist" and that as soon as conditions were right, this particular antisemitism would by its very nature turn to extermination.

Goldhagen professes to have put up this theory in order to be able to explain the German Holocaust. Without that eliminationist antisemitism, he says, the Holocaust could not have happened. The trouble with this reasoning is that it is circular. For without the Holocaust actually being practiced by Germans in the 1940s there is no convincing evidence of its alleged cause: eliminationist antisemitism. Goldhagen is forced into this circularity (special German antisemitism explains Holocaust, Holocaust explains special German antisemitism), because he shuns comparative research into other nations' antisemitisms, which might have proved or falsified his theory.

Yet this insistence on German antisemitism having been eliminationist from the start is by his own terms of reference a non-issue anyway, as he all but admitted in a long article in *Die Zeit* (August 2, 1996). Here, and in the special foreword to the German edition of his book, he stated that there were three conditions for the Holocaust to come about: an antisemitic government ready to exterminate the Jews, an antisemitic populace to follow and provide the willing executioners, and a geopolitical situation allowing such policy to be implemented. He did not mention a general eliminationist antisemitism. Now, these three factors did coincide for Germany (and for no other nation). Where, then, is the need for postulating a German antisemitism different from the common antisemitism in Europe?

Yet Goldhagen repeats this thesis, after his own foreword has undermined it, in about a hundred passages spread over the five hundred pages of his book. Why such irrationality? Could it be a pernicious anti-Germanism in Daniel Goldhagen?

Knowing him from a TV talk show, I suppose that if hard pressed, he might just possibly concede my point, admitting that the essential feature of the Holocaust (genocide) did not need a specific German antisemitism but he would probably still maintain that certain other aspects of it, for instance, the brutality of the perpetrators, would otherwise be inexplicable. He makes a lot of this brutality of the willing executioners in connection with the point that they were ordinary Germans. He insinuates that any ordinary antisemitism could never have led to such brutality. However, excessive brutality is the hallmark of all the pogroms history records, and of course they too were conducted by ordinary Frenchmen, Spaniards, Poles, Russians, etc. Assuming that France or England or Italy or Spain or Poland or Russia had produced a Hitlerite government and got into the geopolitical situation to implement its plans to murder the Jews — what makes him think that these governments would not have found the willing executioners (who he imagines can only be the products of an antisemitism peculiar to Germany)? There is, to my knowledge, not a single instance in history that a government bent on an evil career had to abandon a project because it lacked the soldiers, police, informers, careerists, torturers, and hangmen to put it into practice. They have invariably been forthcoming.

He explains with perfect naivete why he insists on calling the willing executioners not Nazis or SS but Germans — because, he says, that was what they were (p. 6).[47] In reality, of course, he is not stating a fact but making a decision. He argues correctly that al-

---

47 Numbers in parentheses in this and the following letter refer to pages in
   Daniel Goldhagen, *Hitler's Willing Executioners*. Little, Brown and Co. 1995.

though some of those men were Nazi or SS, others were not. But he chooses to overlook, or discount, that while many of them were Germans, others were not (but Lithuanians, Ukrainians, Poles, even Luxembourgers). What then about his explanation of their brutality from an exclusively German antisemitism? He tries to escape this corner saying that, anyway, the prime movers were German. But his book is definitely not about the prime movers, it's about their willing executioners, and the fact that non-Germans as executioners were if anything even more willing than Germans, cannot possibly be explained by who the prime movers were.

Goldhagen applauds himself (p. 9ff.) for being the first who really makes a proper study of the perpetrators. "We must attempt the difficult enterprise of imagining ourselves in their places, performing their deeds, acting as they did…" (p. 21). This would indeed have been an interesting enterprise, especially credible if undertaken by a Jew. Yet how could he hope to succeed in this if for him they are nothing but Germans, categorically "not like us" (p. 27) but belonging to a separate species branded with a pernicious antisemitism foreign to other nations? If he had been serious about understanding them, he might for a start have called them not Germans but Europeans, or whites, or, for that matter, human beings. If he had done that, he might have come up with much less strained and probably more disturbing explanations than his bulldozing German antisemitism.

He also never considers the possibility that the fact that they all were police may have some bearing on the relative uniformity of their willingness. He uncritically assumes that in such circumstances men, ordered to round up, kill, or deport Jews and, not being beset by that specially pernicious German antisemitism, would disobey orders, ask for transfer, or would at least avoid all unnecessary brutality while doing what was required of them.

But before isolating a special German antisemitism, a historian ought to think again and look at other instances of army and police brutality, blissfully killing, torturing helpless, innocent people. The Jew and former communist Lew Kopelew, after reading Goldhagen's book, had some interesting things to say on what the Russians under the czars and in the *gulag* were capable of doing (*Die Zeit*, September 27, 1996), you, James Bacque, in *Other Losses* assembled ample evidence of what American and French soldiers did to Germans after they could be sure that no retaliation was to be expected; and John Sack had a tale to tell of what Jews did to Germans after the war in Poland.[48] The emergence of this phenomenon is in fact of such universal regularity that as researchers after truth, we may have to reconsider our bland notions of Normal-Null under circumstances God save us from ever getting into and having to prove our superior humanity.

I have to overcome some strong resistance before I can bring myself for truth's sake to speak against Goldhagen's assumption that killing people en masse, especially if on command and in the context of a fortifying and like-minded group, needs some extraordinary motivation and cannot be a gratifying pastime in itself. But along with defending your own life, not wishing to be found a coward, or not wanting to let down your comrades (plus the sheer routine of going on with what you do well and have for whatever reason been doing well yesterday and the day before), this joy of killing is something that has kept armies all over the world fighting. Once a war is well under way, higher motivations (patriotism, ideology) count for little with most soldiers. And of course the innate gratification of killing becomes the more perfect the more superior your weapons are, the more helpless the enemy. Allied fighter planes at the end of the Second World War hunted women and children like rabbits all over Germany for weeks on end, and the same joy of the hunt occurred at the end of the last Gulf war. Most youths worldwide stick to video games, but who can doubt the ease of transfer to the real thing when the situation (as in the Balkans recently) arises? Antisemitism or anti-Germanism or anti-collaborationism, or anti-Bosnianism or anti-Iraqi-ism or whatever kind of mindset, of course, helps and is welcome for supporting and camouflaging the gut joy of it, especially when there is still some kind of stink about it, as there was, I would maintain, in the case of the Jews. The same label of normality must unfortunately be accorded also to brutality as it emerges under certain well-known police conditions — to be curbed only by strictly enforced discipline or by a statistically rare unshakeable morality. It seems we have to acknowledge a deep-down necessity for this brutality in the case of

48 John Sack: *An Eye for an Eye: The Untold Story of Jewish Revenge Against Germans in 1945*. NY 1993. Under public pressure, the 6000 copies of the German translation were destroyed by the publisher Piper before publication.

police or police-like troops, guarding masses of people in a restricted place (concentration camps, prisons), when in your minority position of authority you feel the need to intimidate your wards, or, in the case of executions, the need to degrade and torture them before you can kill with equanimity, especially if asked to do it face-to-face.

The ideal exterminator as envisaged by the puritan Himmler (and also somehow by Goldhagen himself), the clean, disinterested male who heroically overcomes his aversion to the job every day anew for the purpose of some accepted higher Good, is, it seems, a human impossibility. This also applies to attendant symptoms of those horrors. As the clearest proof that these ordinary people must have been driven by some demonic German hatred of Jews, Goldhagen cites their making fun of the victims, their taking snapshots, their boasting and feasting. But he himself inadvertently points to the parallel with medical students' regularly enjoying their unsavoury insider jokes at the expense of moribunds and corpses they are learning to live with.

Goldhagen's inability to really understand what happened in the police battalions is starkly clear in his interpretation of the volunteer syndrome. He shows that some officers told their men that they could with impunity excuse themselves from the killings. This, as he rightly says, does away with the idea of these men being mere automatons, blindly following orders. Yet, without his noticing, it also does away with his grand theory of their being possessed by a burning eliminationist antisemitism, which, if true, would make such volunteer subtleties pointless. But that apart, difficult commandos in any army of the world have always depended on volunteers. Offering a way out will call up a man's feeling of personal honour. As one of the policemen said, and Goldhagen quotes him, "One does not want to be considered a coward."

But there is more to Goldhagen's decision to make "the" Germans the German nation, German society and so on, the grammatical subject of all his hundreds of sentences stating what was done to the Jews (echoing Yitzhak Shamir's absurd statement in an American TV interview on November 15, 1988: that "the great majority of the German people *decided to murder* millions of Jews").

Goldhagen unfolds the history of German antisemitism over the centuries down to the twelve years of Hitler's rule. He starts with the Middle Ages, proceeds via Martin Luther and comes into his own in the nineteenth century with the breaking-up of the Jewish ghetto and the Jews' civic emancipation. Following almost exclusively one source (a German dissertation by Konrad Felden of 1963), he not only sees the emergence of a more general, less Christian-oriented antisemitism (which is okay), but also finds his pet theory confirmed that it was a particularly nasty kind of antisemitism. He simply quotes from Felden's quotations of shocking German publications and tracts, impressing his readers with figures (twelve hundred such publications from 1870 to 1900), which he supposes leave no doubt as to the impact they made on the German reading public. Although he admits that to us they look and sound idiotic, he never addresses the question of whether he may have got hold of what even then was a lunatic fringe. The fact that the readers of this trash and their antisemitic parties were never able to induce any Wilhelmian governments to introduce anti-Jewish measures is played down. He also never asks himself how the disproportionate economic and social rise of the 1 per cent of Jews in Germany's total population, their enormous success in business, law, and medicine could have taken place without the active support of the non-Jewish German customers and clients, and how that would fit his idea of their pernicious antisemitism.

And the same applies even more to the Weimar years. He ignores the balanced account of this period in Sarah A. Gordon's excellent work on German antisemitism although he knows the book and refers to it on two points between 1933 and 1945.[49] He has to admit that even for the 33.1 per cent of the overall vote, which in the last free elections were cast for Hitler's party, antisemitism played a minor role; but he draws no conclusions from this for his main tenet of raging Jew-hatred in Germany. In fact between 1930 and 1933 Hitler's election campaign propaganda avoided antisemitism as being counter-productive. Only 15 per cent of SA storm troopers joined up because the SA was antisemitic.

And what about the time after 1933? Goldhagen maintains in ever more hectoring tones that owing to Nazi government propaganda "the" Germans became even more perniciously antisemitic and ready to approve and support the extermination of the Jews. He even goes so far as to state (p. 8) that from then on antisemitism was

---

49 Sarah A. Gordon, *Hitler, Germans and the "Jewish Question"*. Princeton NJ 1984.

nothing less than "the [!] defining feature of German society". (This is one of the places where his German translator baulked, replacing "the" by "a").

My own memory tells me that apart perhaps from children and students, at least in my Catholic Rhineland, the Nazis failed to make the normal German more antisemitic than he or she had traditionally been. Peter Wyden, in his biography (1993) of Stella (the glamorous Jewish Gestapo stool pigeon) writes of himself and his family: "Besides, we German Jews believed to be at anchor in a safe harbour. In a pretty tolerant environment, they did not have the feeling of being different. ... My father's ancestors had for ages been small businessmen in rural regions of Germany. Should he feel expelled, because rowdies defaced shop windows with saucy slogans? Ridiculous!"[50] Or, among others, Saul Friedlander: "The *NSDAP*** must have soon realized that anti-Semitism had not much mobilization effect, rather the contrary," and "There was no mass movement against the Jews, not even a crusade by a fanatical sect."[51] (Saul Friedlander: "Vom Antisemitismus zur Judenvernichtung," in: Jäckel/Rohwer, *Der Mord an den Juden im Zweiten Weltkrieg*, 1987, p. 38 and 48). In fact, Hitler here, as in the field of foreign policy, became the victim of his own successes. Just as the majority of Germans to my memory were perfectly happy with the Saar, Austria, and the Sudetenland back where they belonged (and quite unwilling to risk war for anything beyond — which, by the way, was also Goering's view), the normal antisemitic German, if he or she still took an interest in the "Jewish Question" at all after the Jews had been taken down a peg or two, saw no reason to go on pestering them. Even now I find it unrealistic to suppose that, all the evidence of continuing antisemitic Nazi propanda notwithstanding, sloganeering and hate speeches could have impressed the ordinary German any further.

As I remember clearly, and this is borne out by later events in communist countries with comparable propaganda efforts directed at capitalists and aristocrats, people just paid attention no longer,

---

* (National-Sozialistische Deutsche Arbeiter-Partei — Hitler's party)
50 Peter Wyden, *Stella*, Göttingen 1993, p. 49 (R.'s translation).
51 Saul Friedlander — Jew, emigrated to England.

and quite a few were positively sick of it. As the taking of Prague in 1939 was seen as a first false step beyond the limit of correcting Versailles, the staging of Kristallnacht of 1938 by Goebbels was generally regarded as a wanton brutality. The war, when it had in people's belief been forced on Germany by Polish insouciance, took everybody's mind even further off the Jews who before the Star of David was introduced had become practically invisible to the rest of the population (and the Star, as Jews have witnessed, roused more irritation and pity than hate in most people). Goebbels, according to Speer, remarked to Hitler at the end of 1941, "Mein Führer! We wanted to exclude the Jews from the German people (*Volksgemeinschaft*). But the common people do not avoid them — on the contrary! Everywhere they show sympathy to them. This people is simply not yet mature, is full of sloppy sentimentalism (*Gefühlsduselei*)[52]; And Hitler himself, after the Wannsee Conference of January 20, 1942, in one of his Table Talks, made fun of his Germans: "If today I remove the Jew, our bourgoisie is unhappy: What's happening to him?"[53]

Goldhagen omits or dismisses this and other evidence that might prove him wrong. He quotes only a few German Jews who seem to support his ideas. But if antisemitism was indeed a defining feature of German society, it must have been of a kind compatible with all the anecdotal evidence against its perniciousness. It must especially be compatible with certain more general facts. While on average twenty-three thousand Jews left Germany annually between 1933 and 1938, four times as many left much smaller Poland every year during the same period; and after the SA campaign against them had subsided, ten thousand returned (!) to Germany. Could they have been that blind to a specially pernicious antisemitism in their neighbours? And that in 1934? Goldhagen postulates that anti-Jewish politics, and by implication politics in general, dominated the life of ordinary Germans. As if a whole nation, with the possible exception of total war, could be turned into a mere instrument of a government — and that within the short time Hitler had at his disposal! To the great mass of Germans, as to most people of the

---

52 Albert Speer, *Spandauer Tagebücher*. Frankfurt am Main 1975, p. 401.
53 Adolf Hitler, *Monologe im Führerhauptquartier 1941-1944. Die Aufzeichnungen Heinrich Heims*, ed. Werner Jochmann. Hamburg, 1980, p. 228. (R.'s translation). US edition: *Hitler's Secret Conversations 1941-1944*. NY 1961.

world, politics was but one thin stratum of their lives, now and then interfering with what mainly occupied their minds: their jobs, their businesses, their love affairs, their pastimes, their wives and husbands, their children and relatives, sports and other club activities. It takes people in the media, political writers, leading figures in the parties to make politics their life concern.

Even the Nazi youth organization, which I was a member of, was not dominated by Nazism, but by being young together, by field games, by hiking, tenting, singing, the usual Baden-Powell stuff. No youth organization of whatever political or religious stripe has ever been able to survive on a different diet. Explicit propaganda and sloganeering wear off quickly. People found Hitler's long speeches boring, not to speak of the efforts of the smaller Nazi fry. Nazi hatred of the Jews was taken for granted, and it is true that most people thought there was cause for it, but to imagine that this dominated their thinking in those years is a fallacy in the young historian Goldhagen, who, curiously, is quite aware of this fallacy in other historians when he treats the everyday lives of the police battalions. The Jewish professor Victor Klemperer in his diaries time and again wonders how little non-Jewish Germans knew of what kind of life Jews among them were forced to live; even the German officials he had to deal with could not believe the ever tighter restrictions that were visited on Dresden Jews and Jews everywhere by the Gestapo.[54]

This professor, who, although deprived of his university post, thanks to a non-Jewish wife managed to stay on in Dresden and over the twelve years of Hitler's rule kept writing this diary of thousands of pages "in order to be able to give evidence to the last." As it is an inquisitive day-to-day account of what the Klemperers and all the Jews they knew did and thought and suffered, and as it was never tampered with afterwards, neither by the writer nor anybody else, it is especially reliable. In my count, of the fifty-two passages recording ordinary Germans' reactions in deed or word to Nazism and the Jews, seventeen are pro-Nazi/anti-Jewish, and more than double that number (thirty-seven) anti-Nazi/pro-Jewish. (In eleven places he records pro-Nazi remarks by Jews.) His account is definitely unsuitable for whitewashing the Germans of their antisemitism, but in its

Victor Klemperer, *Ich will Zeugnis ablegen bis zum letzten, Tagebücher 1933-1941*, Berlin 1995, Vol II, 553. — *I Will Bear Witness 1941 - 1945: A Diary of the Nazi Years.* Vol. II, NY: Random House 1999.

principled objectivity it is strong evidence against Goldhagen's idea of a widespread incomparably pernicious antisemitism of the Germans in those years.

Dear Jim, if today's German public were still unable to grasp what indeed far too many of them or their parents and grandparents did to the European Jews, if they hadn't in fact proved to be the only nation in history to repent collectively, one might, in spite of all I have been saying, still welcome a book that in many of its pages has the force of a baroque penitential sermon. However, it comes at a time when the German expiation movement after roughly forty years of growth has entered a dubious triumphalist phase, and what is needed now is, I think, sober thought, serious corrective scholarship, serving a new togetherness of nations. As Val Williams in the *New Statesman* recently (November 24, 1995) said, "It's easy to make people feel guilty, it's quite another thing to make them think."

R.

May 3, 1996

Dear Richard,

Congratulations on being able to take Goldhagen's book seriously. Or perhaps that should be sympathy at having to do so. It is a weird mixture of hate literature and comical ineptitude. Like the work of antisemites, it is animated by resentment of a racial/ethnic group rather than by interest in history. I resent Goldhagen also because he has fanned my embered hatred of Germans and given me new but spurious reasons for it. And we were getting along so well, you and I....

You report that Goldhagen says that as "soon as conditions were right," German antisemitism would by its very nature turn to extermination. But when the Germans ruled western Russia, including Poland, for years during the Great War, there was no pogrom there. Surely, if Goldhagen were correct, and Germans were from time out of mind so murderously antisemitic, then the kaiser's government would have been just as infected as Hitler's with the desire to exterminate the Jews. After all, the kaiser was a well-known racist, inventor of the term "The Yellow Peril," and his government had not only won the war in the East but had signed a peace treaty. Presumably, in 1917 and later, they felt even safer to do the dirty deeds than Hitler did after 1941. But no, there was none of that.

What struck me above all is that the book is so ugly. His lugubrious inventions go from single neologisms, like biologized *to sentences like "In Nazi Germany, affirmation of 'race' as an organizing principle of social and political life was to accept the foundation of the regnant cultural cognitive model of Jews, since the two are intertwined." (p. 115) Like the title, most of his chapter titles have a colon in the middle, digesting nothing, but producing a little squirm of words beyond — the subtitle. He also loves that fashionable academic solecism, the Siamese-twin phrase joined at the* as. *For instance, Eliminationist Antisemitism* as *Genocidal Motivation. He certainly needed an Eliminationist Editor* as *Extirpatory Grammarian.*

My favourite among his hilarious boners arises because the poor booby thinks that wizened *means "made wise." "The men of Police Battalion 65 were particularly wizened to the nature of Jewish 'resettlement.'" (p. 199) This is perhaps because "a personnel change demarcated the battalion's two instantations," while they were "operationalizing..." so they could "utterly decimate" Jews, along with the English language.*

He believes that "genocide was immanent in the conversation of German society. It was immanent in its language and emotion. It was immanent in the structure of cognition." (p. 449) Now, because immanent *is so important in this context, let's look in the Oxford. And there we see "inherent...permanently pervading..." Thus in plain terms he is saying that genocide was inherent in the conversation of Germans, that it pervaded every aspect of language and emotion. This means it was normally present in both love and hate, in laughter and sadness, in regret and hope. It means that genocide was approved in every conversation that had to do with auto mechanics, making wurst, or making love. It even infected their deep discussions of "their structure of cognition," not to mention the ignition of their cars.*

He is so intent on his thesis that he slurs even the Germans of the resistance who saved Jews from the Nazi terror. "If it can be shown that even the 'friends' of the Jews concurred with German antisemites about essential aspects of their understanding of the Jews' nature,...then it would be difficult to believe anything but that antisemitism was endemic to German culture and society." Although he writes correctly of Berthold von Stauffenberg, the brother of Claus, who planted the bomb at Rastenburg: "[to Berthold]...The concept of race seemed sound and very promising..." (p. 306), he suppresses the fact that after witnessing Nazi racist terror, Berthold changed his mind. Far from approving the Nazis' racist principles in 1944, Berthold von Stauffenberg opposed them, at the risk of his life. He was arrested and interrogated for complicity in the attack on the racist Nazi leader, and he ended his statement to police with the words "The fundamental ideas of National Socialism have in practice all been perverted into their opposites."[55]

More powerful evidence against Goldhagen is in a letter written in 1943 by one of the heroes of the resistance, Helmuth James von Moltke:

> *But even in Germany people do not know what is happening. I believe that at least 9tenths [sic] of the population do not know that we have killed hundreds of thousands of jews [sic].... the opposition is saving individual lives. We can not prevent the ferocious orders from being given, but we can save individuals. And this is done in all walks of life. People who have been officially executed still live, others have been given sufficient warning to escape in time. This is especially so in occupied countries: there is no denying the mass murders, but once the balance is drawn, people will perhaps realize that many thousands of lives have been saved by the intervention of some German, sometimes a private and sometimes a general, sometimes a workman and sometimes a high-ranking official.[56]*

Here is significant proof that the Nazis had to hide their eliminations from the "eliminationist" Germans. Since Germans up to that point had been winning the war, there was no question of retribution. What explanation can there be for hiding what Goldhagen says all Germans secretly approved? Except that they disapproved.

Finally, here are the words of the head of the State Secret Police commission, which investigated the July 1944 assassination attempt on Hitler. The head, SS Lt.-Col. Walter von Kielpinski, wrote, "The complete inner alienation from the idea of National Socialism which characterized the men of the reactionary conspiratorial [Stauffenberg] circle expresses itself above all in their position on the Jewish Question. ... [T]hey cling to the liberal position of granting to the Jews in principle the same status as to every German."[57]

If it is true that some of the Germans in the resistance disliked Jews, it is clear that some of these Germans rose above their petty animosities to obey the noble Christian injunctions "Love thy neighbour," "Turn the

---

55 Peter Hoffmann, *Stauffenberg.* Cambridge, 1995, p 68.
56 Helmuth James von Moltke, *Letters to Freya,* edited and translated by Beate Ruhm von Oppen, Knopf, 1990, p. 285-287.
57 Peter Hoffmann, ibid., p. XIV.

*other cheek," and "Do good to those who hurt you." Goldhagen's flimsy
case for the endemic nature of antisemitism also demonstrates his triviality, since the prejudice disappeared immediately on encountering the lethal extension that Goldhagen pretends was inevitable in Germany.*

*I thought that we in Canada had laws against hate literature. Certainly, they have been used before. One visiting British historian, David
Irving, was arrested and taken to a plane in handcuffs, forbidden ever to
return, ostensibly for a minor infraction of Canadian immigration regulations. The general belief in Canada however is that he was deported for
questioning the statistics of the Holocaust. Irving has denied this accusation categorically. He has said, "I was not arrested for questioning the
statistics of the Holocaust; one of the lies planted on the Canadian
Government computer was that I had written books denying the Holocaust. This is simply not the truth."*

*Others, notably school teachers, have lost their jobs because they were
alleged to have incited people to hatred by denying the tragedy of the Jews.
Now a writer on the west coast is being harassed for the same thing.
Clearly, revisionists are under attack and severely punished when they
express their opinions on the subject.*

*Here we have to ask, what exactly is a revisionist? What does he or she
actually do? The answer is fairly simple: under Section 319 of the Criminal Code of Canada, covering public incitement to hatred, a revisionist is
anyone who denies that the Germans killed as many as six million Jews
during the war. This diminishment is the hatred, is the "crime." It is seen
as sufficient justification to kick a person out of the country, or to fire
him from his job, and to deny him any public forum in the whole country.
This man, however deluded, would not be attacking anyone, but simply
defending Germans against what he regards as a slander. In simple
language then, so far as these terrible charges are concerned, it is a crime
in Canada and Germany to defend Germans. That it seems to me would
be unreasonable, if the law did not also assume or imply, or were interpreted to mean, that as a result of such a defence of Germans there would
be a serious danger to Canadian citizens. What would that danger be?
As I understand the position of Holocaust believers, to allow free speech
and free doubt on the matter might bring down the wrath of a large
section of the Canadian population on the heads of Jews, who would —
IF the Holocaust revisionists were believed — be accused of a vast scam
and a vast sham.*

*Allow for a moment the reasonable assumption that not many Jews
would inhibit free speech merely because they might be insulted — which
after all happens to many Canadians, including separatists, federalists,*

Reform politicians, lawyers, aborigines, oriental immigrants, policemen, the wealthy, the elite. And let us further imagine that after a free debate, the revisionists were once more discredited, what then? Obviously no harm is done, except to them. But suppose for a moment that the revisionists somehow got a significant measure of popular support, what then? Can we imagine what would be worse than the insult? The assumption here must be that non-Jewish Canadians, outraged by the scam, would deport Jews, or attack their buildings, or refuse to do business with them, or whatever.

Is there such a latent, widespread antisemitism?

There have recently been many events which antisemites might have tried to use to foment resentment against Jews not only in Canada but throughout the English-speaking world. In England Robert Maxwell with his brokers at Goldman Sachs and Eric P. Sheinberg; in the U.S. Ivan Boesky and Michael Milken; the Reichmann family of Toronto and Julius Melnitzer of London, Ontario. And yet in fifty years, I have never heard any criticism of Jews or Judaism in even the most private corners of exclusive clubs in Toronto or in old established Anglican families of Ontario.

The most antisemitic things I have heard in fifty years of life among the establishment of eastern Canada have been, and this only lately, expressions of weariness or exasperation with the repetition of the holocaust theme, and a certain fatigue at what is perceived to be constant propaganda for Israel and Jews in general through the media. I could not measure this, but to me it seems of roughly the same kind as the attitudes of the Canadians towards say Ireland and the troubles there, and the incessant repetition of Celtic music and so on right now in the press and TV. We all want to say, "It is enough, end the hatred, let us hear and read something else." It was precisely this feeling that animated me to write the story of how Raoul Laporterie stood almost alone against the Nazi tyrants, showing us the path of best resistance while also saving the lives of more than a thousand refugees, chiefly Jews from Bordeaux.

And just here let me coax out of the closet the best-kept secret on this subject. It is this: Christians and Jews are getting on just fine in this country, and have done for generations. In Voices of Canadian Jews, *a book edited by Jews, about Jewish contributions to Canada, prominent on the first page are the words, "This book...is a paean to Canada."*[58]

---

58 Edited by Bryan M. Knight and Rachel Alkallay, The Chessnut Press, Montreal.

Jews are prominent or dominant in lots of fields, and no-one gainsays them. We like and dislike each other for our personal characteristics, our children are friends, there is a fair rate of intermarriage, and although conservatives on either side worry about such young love and complain about it, and are prejudiced against it, usually, love and desire conquer all, and new people are born who further unite us. But regardless of marriage, our friendships are deep and old. We go into business together, we act on the same stages, make films and music together, teach and learn from each other and so on without the least prejudice against religion, race, ethnic background or whatever.

This is a state of affairs that most of us are content with. And I say with a growl of warning, "God and the law damn anyone who tries to incite hatred and fears between these two befriending peoples." I hate revisionists who are antisemites to insult the Jews. I hate to see anyone trying to split my precious society by setting group against group. But for the same reason I hate to see Germans as a group routinely abused.

If it is true that in the interests of free speech, we must let people like Goldhagen preach hatred against Germans, then in the interests of free speech, we should allow others to defend them. Our American cousins allow David Irving and others like him to go about making speeches questioning the received opinion of the holocaust, and so far, the U.S. is pogrom-free.

The worst hate-violence here is always against women and children, against orientals and recent immigrants from almost anywhere, and the pervasive, endemic apparently hopeless racism against aborigines. And against Germans.

A Canadian cabinet minister of German origin was called "A Nazi" by a caller to a Winnipeg radio talk show. The Minister was descended from people who arrived in Canada six generations before. That this insult was judged and found to be acceptable to broadcast is shown by the fact that on such radio talk shows, a station editor monitors every call for obscenity and racial slurs during an eight-second tape delay. A man born in Germany who was a candidate for mayor of a big Canadian city was defeated after a whispering campaign urging people to ask themselves "what uniform was (candidate) wearing in 1945?" In fact, he was five years old.

Immigrants of German origin have for years been accused of war crimes, then found innocent, then harassed about alleged technicalities on immigration papers which no longer exist. The Canadian government has hired as a special adviser on such alleged war crimes matters a man who was formerly associated with the U.S. Department of Justice, whose officials were found to have perpetrated a fraud on the U.S court, for producing false papers to convict John Demjanjuk of war crimes. It took the high good sense of the Israeli Supreme Court to undo that horrifying wrong, yet here in Canada the government is grimly going down the same road again. To get Germans.

Anna Tuerr of Kitchener has said that she suffered in silence for forty years while her children were abused and mocked in school, her country- men were vilified and lost business because of constant anti-German hatred in the press and TV. She spoke out finally not in resentment of the critics, but because she wanted her children to know the truth of her suffering in the post-war period in Europe, where she lost most of her family after the war. *They died during the brutal ethnic cleansing and starvation imposed by the allies, including Britain, France, Canada and the US. But for thirty years, there was absolutely nothing about this in any of the western media, whereas German crimes were constantly dis- played, ten, twenty, a thousand times over, often with wild exaggerations. Only recently have a few books and newspaper stories begun to tell of the vengeful violence inflicted on Germans after 1945.*

Another woman, born in Poland in 1940, highly educated, now living in North America, has been so hurt by her frequent encounters with anti- German hatred in Poland, then in Canada at school, university, on TV, in the press, at parties, in books and in her professional life, that when she was about forty, she found herself unable to speak about anything personal at all. She could speak or write only a little, and only about her professional work. She could not write a personal letter to a friend. Friend- ship, love, art — most of the joys that make life worth living — were denied her by this shamed silence that suddenly overwhelmed her. She had to undergo years of painful therapy to discover the cause, and the cure. Her younger sister, who suffered similar wounds, has been in a mental home in Canada for over thirty years, completely silent. They have been silenced by the unremitting prejudice against them.

All of these hurt people were either old-family Canadians or they were small children during the war. And that is true of nearly all Germans in Germany today — they were children during the war, or were born after 1945. Surely after fifty years, we can find it in our hearts to forgive the innocent.

Well, Richard, here we are at a goodbye again, having often said "Goodbye" and "Auf Wiedersehen," — in Bad Kreuznach, Toronto,

Monschau and Monschau again, then in Mexico. So now I say, "Au revoir," old friend, and I look forward to seeing you again soon, in Kanada.

J.

June 6, 1996

Dear Jim,

Last time you were with us here you left me the novel *Away* by Jane Urquhart. It's only now that I have come around to reading it. As its narrative moved from Ireland to Canada, memories of you and your country came crowding back to me. And then your proud Goldhagen letter arrived, shortly before I got to page 174 in the Urquahart book. There, with the Ojibwa talking about the crow, who is his "spirit-guide," I thought to myself, Isn't that native of Canada conjuring up the very spirit of James Bacque? "He is a wise bird who survives hardships and who loves that which shines. He is a bird with a strong voice who insists on being heard. Because he sits high on the top branch of the tallest tree in the forest, and flies even higher than that, he can see many things at once and so is a good guide. Because he flies fast and calls loudly he is a good messenger."

Well, my good messenger, I hope that your messages will always fall on keen, perceptive ears.

R.

DEMCO